# The
# CROSS STITCH
# Motif Bible

Over 1000 motifs with
easy-to-follow color charts

D1364581

## JAN EATON
### CHARTS BY CAROL AND JOHN WOODCOCK

CHARTWELL
BOOKS, INC.

A QUARTO BOOK

This edition published in 2011 by
**CHARTWELL BOOKS, INC.**
A division of BOOK SALES, INC.
276 Fifth Avenue, Suite 206
New York, New York 10001
USA

ISBN-13: 978-0-7858-2865-5

QUAR.CSBI

Conceived, designed, and produced by
Quarto Publishing plc
The Old Brewery
6 Blundell Street
London N7 9BH

**Project editor** Susie May
**Senior art editor** Penny Cobb
**Designers** Sheila Volpe, Carol Woodcock
**Illustrators** Coral Mula (pages 17–23),
    Carol and John Woodcock (pages 30–249)
**Proofreader** Tracie Davis
**Indexer** Geraldine Beare
**Art director** Moira Clinch
**Publisher** Paul Carslake

Color separation by Modern Age Repro House Ltd,
Hong Kong
Printed by Midas printing International Limited,
China

10 9 8 7 6 5 4 3 2 1

# CONTENTS

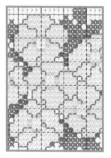

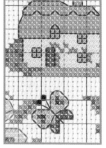

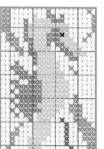

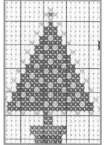

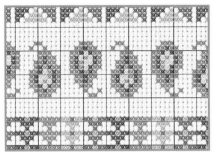

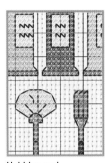

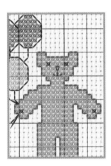

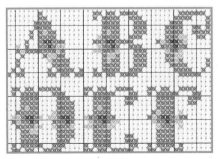

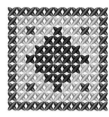

# Introduction

Cross stitch is a very easy embroidery technique to work, and it quickly becomes addictive. To help you quench that addiction this book features over one thousand charted cross stitch designs, including alphabets, motifs, borders, and all-over patterns. The designs have been grouped together in the Pattern Library, which is split into separate sections for ease of use, however you can of course mix and match motifs and borders from any of the sections, and add lettering and numbers. *The Cross Stitch Motif Bible* gives the cross stitcher an almost limitless choice of combinations, so you can truly personalize your stitching.

## Putting it all together

There are many ways that you can use the charts in this book to create unique, individual works of embroidery. You can pick out preferred motifs, styles of lettering, and borders and put them all together using the guidelines in Design Tips (*see page 23*). You can use the colors I have suggested or put together your own combinations. Finally, you can make your works of embroidery into any number of different finished items.

The palette of 58 colors used for the charts is based on the DMC floss range. A list of actual code numbers and color names is provided on page 254, accompanied by their nearest Anchor floss equivalents. Please feel free to experiment with your own color combinations, adding specialty threads, metallic threads, and beads to create the exact effect to suit you.

◊ WEDDING HEARTS
TOM PUDDING DESIGNS
Flowers, bold initials, and a large heart motif combine to make a simple yet effective sampler to commemorate a wedding.

◊ SMALL MOTIF SAMPLER
TOM PUDDING DESIGNS
A selection of traditional
sampler motifs are
contained within a narrow
border to make this
pleasing arrangement.
Tiny silver-colored metal
charms are added
to the design.

Many cross stitchers choose white, cream, or ecru fabric as the background for their stitching, and pale, neutral shades show off the thread colors well, but don't forget that there is a wide variety of other color choices that you can explore. Bright, hot colors can make a simple design look very up-to-the-minute, and dark colors show off an intricately stitched pattern to great effect.

You can also be adventurous when turning your pieces of cross stitch into finished items. Traditional framed samplers are undoubtedly beautiful, as are cross-stitch decorated pillowcases, but perhaps you would prefer to use your embroidery in a whole new way. You could try: stitching a selection of brightly colored fruit motifs (see pages 58–63) on coarse evenweave linen and mounting it in a sleek modern frame to display in a dining area; repeating rows of tiny motifs, such as the smaller butterflies on pages 73–75, on lengths of Aida or linen band and sewing them onto table and bed linen; or mounting your stitching in a box lid or on the front of a simple fabric bag. Even tiny pieces of cross stitch can look lovely made into a pincushion, scissors keeper, or perfumed lavender bag.

Whatever you decide, I hope you enjoy choosing and stitching the designs in the book and that you are ultimately delighted with the finished results.

# 8

# How to use this book

The first section of this book takes you through the materials and techniques needed for working cross stitch embroidery, before moving on to the Pattern Library, which contains over 1,000 motifs for cross stitch with integral color keys. Motif sizes and thread details are then given at the end of the library.

From choosing fabric and threads to working the stitches, each technique is explained in easy-to-follow steps.

The techniques are accompanied by step-by-step photographs and illustrations.

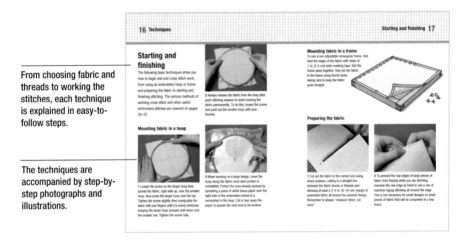

16 Techniques

Starting and finishing 17

## Starting and finishing

The following basic techniques show you how to begin and end cross stitch work, from using an embroidery hoop or frame and preparing the fabric to starting and finishing stitching. The various methods of working cross stitch and other useful embroidery stitches are covered on pages 20–22.

2 Always release the fabric from the hoop after each stitching session to avoid marking the fabric permanently. To do this, loosen the screw and push out the smaller hoop with your thumbs.

### Mounting fabric in a hoop

1 Loosen the screw on the larger hoop then spread the fabric, right side up, over the smaller hoop. Now press the larger hoop over the top. Tighten the screw slightly then manipulate the fabric with your fingers until it is evenly stretched, keeping the larger hoop pressed well down over the smaller one. Tighten the screw fully.

3 When working on a large design, move the hoop along the fabric once each portion is completed. Protect the area already worked by spreading a piece of white tissue paper over the right side of the embroidery before it is remounted in the hoop. Cut or tear away the paper to expose the next area to be worked.

### Mounting fabric in a frame

To use a non-adjustable rectangular frame, first bind the edges of the fabric with strips of 1-in. (2.5-cm) wide masking tape. Slot the frame sides together, then pin the fabric to the frame using thumb tacks, taking care to keep the fabric grain straight.

### Preparing the fabric

1 Cut out the fabric to the correct size using sharp scissors, cutting in a straight line between the fabric blocks or threads and allowing at least a 3–4-in. (8–10-cm) margin of unworked fabric all around the planned design. Remember to always "measure twice, cut once."

2 To prevent the raw edges of large pieces of fabric from fraying while you are stitching, oversew the raw edge by hand or use a row of machine zigzag stitching all around the edge. This is not necessary for small designs on small pieces of fabric that will be completed in a few hours.

## READING A CHART

A cross stitch design is worked from a chart onto evenweave fabric by counting the blocks or threads in the fabric to position the stitches accurately. Each cross stitch is represented in this book by a colored cross occupying one block of fabric. Unfilled fabric blocks on a motif, letter, or border show the number of unworked blocks that separate groups of stitches. As a general rule, start stitching at the center of a cross stitch design, working outward from the center of the chart by working one complete cross stitch for every colored cross shown on the chart.

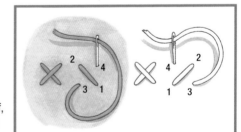

FORMING THE STITCHES Each cross can be formed exactly as shown above left, or the top and bottom diagonal stitches can be worked to slant in the opposite direction as shown above right. Whichever way you prefer to stitch, remember to be consistent, making sure the top diagonals of each cross slant in the same direction.

CATEGORY The motifs are divided into 11 different themes.

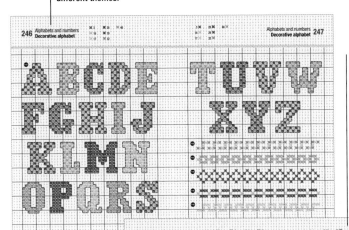

STITCH COLOR KEY A key runs across the top of each page and indicates which thread color should be used to stitch each cross shown on the chart. Fifty-eight colors are used throughout the book and each color is cross-referenced to both DMC and Anchor floss manufacturer numbers on page 254.

NUMBERS Each motif is numbered and cross-referenced to the list of motif sizes at the back of the book.

BACKGROUND GRID To make counting easier, the background grid on each page is divided by thin black lines into blocks of five squares by five.

BACKSTITCH LINES are used to outline and define areas of cross stitch and these are shown as straight stitches on the charts.

FRENCH KNOTS are tiny, raised stitches that add detail and are often used to depict an eye on a bird or animal. They are shown on the charts as tiny solid dots.

# What you will need

Cross stitch does not demand an expensive initial outlay to get you started. Fabric, thread, needles, and an embroidery hoop are all you need to begin stitching. You will then find that as you collect unused fabric and extra threads you can build up a useful embroidery kit for future projects.

## Fabric

There are two main varieties of fabric used for cross stitch work, referred to as evenweave and Aida fabrics, although Aida is still evenly woven. Either of these evenweave fabrics make a good choice for cross stitch because the evenly woven warp and weft threads allow the cross stitches to be made of identical size and to be positioned accurately on the fabric.

**Evenweave fabric** Evenweave fabric has the same number of warp and weft threads woven to every 1 in. (2.5cm) of fabric. The number of threads is called the count and this number varies depending on the weight of the individual threads. The most popular sizes are 28- and 36-count, which contain 28 or 36 threads to every 1 in. (2.5cm). Cross stitch is usually worked over pairs of evenweave threads rather than single threads, which means that when you stitch on 28-count evenweave you can fit 14 stitches into 1 in. (2.5cm) of fabric.

Evenweave fabric can be made from linen, cotton, or a blend that may contain synthetic fibers such as polyester.

**Aida fabric** The most popular evenly woven cotton fabric for cross stitch is called Aida, and varies in appearance to the traditional evenweave fabric described above. For Aida, groups of even-sized threads are woven together to produce a series of distinct blocks, over which individual stitches are worked. The blocks are easy to count accurately so this fabric is perfect for a beginner. Like traditional evenweave, Aida is available in different counts: 14-count Aida—14 blocks to 1 in. (2.5cm)—is one of the most widely used sizes, allowing you to fit 14 stitches to every 1 in. (2.5cm) of fabric; 11-count Aida—11 blocks to 1 in. (2.5cm)—has a larger weave so stitches are bigger, while stitches worked on 16- or 18-count are smaller.

◊ LEFT TO RIGHT
26-count evenweave linen, 26-count evenweave cotton, and 32-count evenweave linen.

◊ TOP TO BOTTOM
18-count cream Aida, 14-count beige Aida, 14-count pink Aida, and 14-count cream Aida with lurex.

**Cross stitch bands** Narrow bands of fabric made specifically for cross stitch are available by the yard or meter in various widths. They are useful for trimming items of home furnishing as well as for making small items such as bookmarks and scented sachets. The central portion of the bands is made from either evenweave linen or Aida and the top and bottom edges are prefinished with a decorative edging. The bands can be bought in several colors and they are usually woven with 14 blocks or 28 threads to every 1 in. (2.5cm).

**Fabric counts** Two strawberries (motif 149, page 58) have been stitched in cotton floss on different counts of cross stitch fabric.

▽ SAMPLE 1 was stitched on 11-count Aida fabric using three strands of floss for the cross stitches and two strands for the backstitch outlines.

▽ SAMPLE 2 was stitched on 14-count Aida fabric using two strands of floss for the cross stitches and one strand for the backstitch outlines.

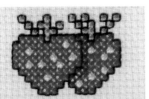

## Threads

Stranded cotton floss is most commonly used for cross stitch, but silk, rayon, specialty, or metallic threads can also be experimented with for varying effects.

**Cotton floss** Cotton floss is the most versatile thread to use for cross stitch. It is available in a wide range of colors and consists of six loosely twisted strands of mercerized cotton. A cut length of floss can be split into different weights to suit different fabric counts. As a general rule, use two strands for stitching on 14-count Aida fabric or over two threads on 28-count evenweave fabric, and three strands for stitching on 11-count Aida fabric. Use floss in 15–18-in. (38–45-cm) lengths to avoid tangling.

▽ SAMPLE 3 was stitched over two threads of 28-count evenweave linen using two strands of floss for the cross stitches and one strand for the backstitch outlines.

▽ SAMPLE 4 was stitched on 16-count Aida using two strands of floss for the cross stitches and one strand for the backstitch outlines.

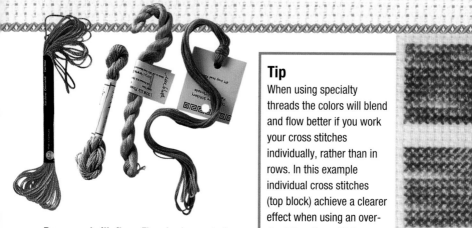

**Rayon and silk floss** Floss is also made from rayon or pure silk. Both types are slightly more expensive but they have a delightful sheen and the colors are vibrant. When using rayon or silk floss, cut a shorter length than usual and choose a tapestry needle with a large enough eye to accommodate the thread comfortably, otherwise it will rub and fray each time you pull the needle through the fabric. Take care to finish off the thread ends carefully when stitching with rayon thread, which is fairly springy.

**Specialty threads** Over-dyed and hand-painted floss, often known as specialty threads, offer a wide range of color mixtures and effects, depending on the manufacturer. Several different shades or colors are applied to the thread at fixed intervals so that they blend into each other. These threads are more expensive than cotton floss in solid colors so should be used in small amounts to add an extra special dash of color to a design.

**Metallic threads** Like specialty threads (*left*) metallic threads can be used to add accents of color and sparkle to a design. They are available in metallic, pearlized, and fluorescent finishes and in varying weights, so choose one

---

> **Tip**
> For just a hint of sparkle, combine a length of blending filament—a very fine metallic thread—with solid cotton floss in the needle.

to suit the count of fabric you are using. Fine braid No. 4 works well on 14-count Aida and 28-count evenweave fabric.

## Needles

Tapestry needles are ideal for use with all evenweave fabrics because their blunt points slide easily through the material without pulling or tearing. These needles are available in different sizes, graded from thick—the low numbers—to fine—the high numbers. The most useful sizes for cross stitch are 24, 26, and 28.

## Hoops and frames

For all but the smallest designs, mounting the fabric in a circular hoop or rectangular frame will help you to stitch evenly and accurately.

Embroidery hoops are available in various sizes and consist of two circular sections placed one inside the other. The fabric is sandwiched between the two sections and secured by a screw at the side. The advantage of using a hoop is that it can be moved across the fabric once each portion of the design has been completed.

Rectangular frames consist of straight wooden bars that slot together and, like hoops,

are available in a good range of sizes. The fabric is attached to the frame using thumb tacks. Unlike a hoop, a frame cannot be moved across the fabric so choose one to suit the size of your work, ensuring that unsightly tack marks do not run into the finished piece.

## Graph paper and design materials

Graph paper is an essential design tool, along with a pen, scissors, and ruler. Using this basic equipment you can choose any number of motifs and combine and space them to create a pleasing arrangement.

## Beads

To add interest to a stitched design you can substitute glass seed beads for some of the cross stitches. Size 11 seed beads fit the weave of 14-count Aida or 28-count evenweave fabric perfectly, so you can apply one bead to one Aida block or pair of evenweave threads. Use a special beading needle or the finest gauge of crewel needle (size 10) to work the stitches when applying beads and match the thread color to the fabric background, not to the color of the bead.

⟡ USING BEADS Green and gold seed beads have been used for the foliage and pips instead of green and yellow cross stitches on these two strawberries (motif 149, page 58) stitched on 14-count Aida using two strands of cotton floss.

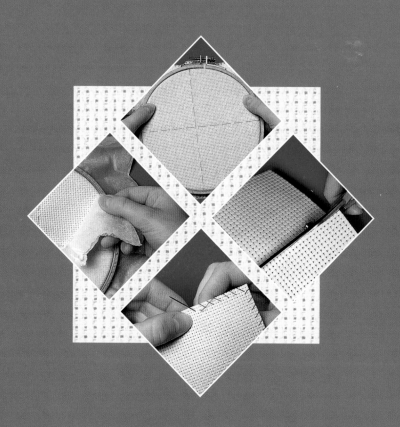

# Chapter

# Techniques

In this chapter, you will find a wealth of expert information to help you start cross stitching, choose fabric and threads, and look after your work. There are also helpful hints on how to use and combine the motifs from the Pattern Library to create your own cross stitch designs.

# Starting and finishing

The following basic techniques show you how to begin and end cross stitch work, from using an embroidery hoop or frame and preparing the fabric to starting and finishing stitching. The various methods of working cross stitch and other useful embroidery stitches are covered on pages 20–22.

**2** Always release the fabric from the hoop after each stitching session to avoid marking the fabric permanently. To do this, loosen the screw and push out the smaller hoop with your thumbs.

## Mounting fabric in a hoop

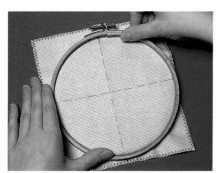

**1** Loosen the screw on the larger hoop then spread the fabric, right side up, over the smaller hoop. Now press the larger hoop over the top. Tighten the screw slightly then manipulate the fabric with your fingers until it is evenly stretched, keeping the larger hoop pressed well down over the smaller one. Tighten the screw fully.

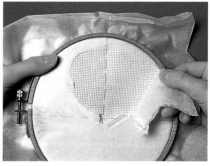

**3** When working on a large design, move the hoop along the fabric once each portion is completed. Protect the area already worked by spreading a piece of white tissue paper over the right side of the embroidery before it is remounted in the hoop. Cut or tear away the paper to expose the next area to be worked.

## Mounting fabric in a frame

To use a non-adjustable rectangular frame, first bind the edges of the fabric with strips of 1-in. (2.5-cm) wide masking tape. Slot the frame sides together, then pin the fabric to the frame using thumb tacks, taking care to keep the fabric grain straight.

## Preparing the fabric

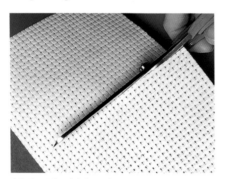

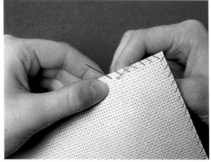

**1** Cut out the fabric to the correct size using sharp scissors, cutting in a straight line between the fabric blocks or threads and allowing at least a 3–4-in. (8–10-cm) margin of unworked fabric all around the planned design. Remember to always "measure twice, cut once."

**2** To prevent the raw edges of large pieces of fabric from fraying while you are stitching, oversew the raw edge by hand or use a row of machine zigzag stitching all around the edge. This is not necessary for small designs on small pieces of fabric that will be completed in a few hours.

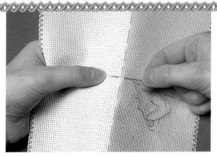

quarters and mark the point where the folds join with a pin. Unfold the fabric and work two rows of basting stitches along the folds so the rows cross at this point. Use a contrasting color of sewing thread for the basting so that the stitches are easy to see. Starting at the center of the fabric, work the group of stitches nearest to the center of the chart. Work the remainder of the design outward from these stitches by counting the squares on the chart to determine the placing of the stitches.

**3** Cross stitch is always worked outward from the center of the design, to ensure there is an even margin of fabric all around the finished piece. To find the center, fold the fabric into

## Starting to stitch

There are several ways to anchor the thread end when you begin stitching, so choose the method that feels most comfortable to you.

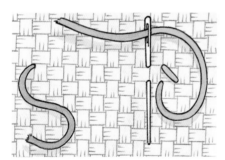

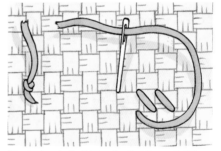

**Loose-end start** Take the needle through to the wrong side of the fabric close to where you intend to start stitching and leave a 2-in. (5-cm) length of thread hanging loose on the surface. Continue stitching until you finish the length of thread (*see* Finishing off the thread, *right*), then return to the loose end, take it through to the wrong side and darn it in under a group of stitches.

**Waste-knot start** Tie a knot at the end of the thread. Take the needle through to the wrong side of the fabric a short distance away from where you will be stitching, so the thread on the back lies along the position of the first few stitches. Work the stitches up to the knot, securing the thread on the back, then carefully snip off the knot.

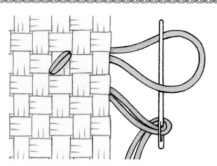

**Loop start** When stitching with an even number of strands of thread you can use the

loop start. Cut the thread twice as long as usual. To loop start when using two strands, simply fold the thread in half and thread the cut ends through the eye of the needle, making a loop at the other end. Bring the needle through the fabric at the beginning of the first stitch and pull the thread through to leave the loop on the wrong side. Make the first stitch, take the needle to the wrong side, slip it through the loop and pull gently to anchor the end.

## Finishing off the thread

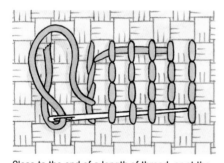

Close to the end of a length of thread, or at the end of a design element, take the needle through to the wrong side of the fabric. Slide the needle through the last few stitches you have worked, pull gently and cut off the thread end. Don't be tempted to carry a length of thread across the wrong side between two stitched areas because this may show through on the right side and spoil the stitching. Instead, fasten off the thread after each area is completed.

## Joining in a new length

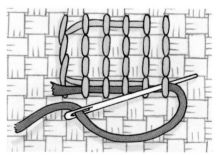

On the wrong side of the fabric, take the new length of thread under the back of several stitches close to where you are stitching. Take a small stitch over the last stitch already worked and bring the needle through the fabric ready to begin stitching.

# The stitches

Cross stitches can be worked individually or in rows. Individual stitches should be used for small areas of color, while rows of stitches are suitable for filling in solid blocks of color. Backstitch and French knots are the other stitches used with cross stitch, to make straight lines or solid dots for eyes, and the stitch for applying beads can also be useful to learn.

## Individual cross stitch

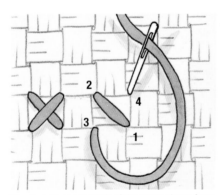

The first diagonal stitch of the cross slants from bottom right to top left. Bring the needle through at 1 and insert it at 2 to make a half-cross stitch. Complete the cross by stitching the second diagonal from bottom left (3) to top right (4). Repeat as required.

## Cross stitch in horizontal rows

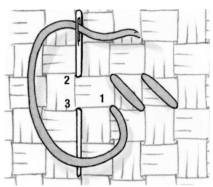

**1** Each row of crosses is worked over two horizontal journeys. On the first journey, work from right to left making a row of evenly spaced diagonal stitches. Bring the needle through at 1 and insert it at 2. Bring the needle through at 3, ready to make the next stitch at the left. Repeat as required along the row.

**2** At the end of the row, turn and work back in the opposite direction making diagonal stitches to complete the crosses. Insert the needle at 4 and bring it through at 5. Work the next and subsequent rows below the first and repeat until the block of color is completed.

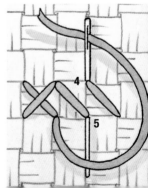

## Cross stitch in vertical rows

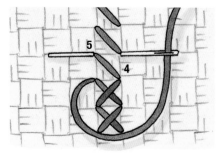

**1** Each row of crosses is worked over two vertical journeys. On the first journey, work from top to bottom making a row of evenly spaced diagonal stitches. Bring the needle through at 1 and insert it at 2. Bring the needle through at 3, ready to make the next stitch below. Repeat as required along the row.

**2** At the end of the row, work back in the opposite direction making diagonal stitches to complete the crosses. Insert the needle at 4 and bring it through at 5. Work the next and subsequent rows at the left of the first and repeat until the block of color is completed.

## Backstitch

Work backstitch from right to left, making straight stitches forward and backward along the row. Bring the needle through at 1 and insert it to the right at 2, then bring it through again at 3. To make the next stitch, insert the needle at the left-hand end of the previous stitch. Backstitches may be vertical, horizontal, or diagonal and cover one or more fabric blocks.

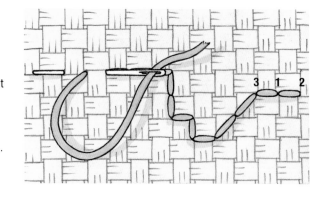

## French knots

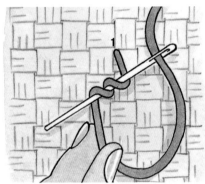

**1** Bring the needle through at 1. Holding the thread taut with your left hand, twist the needle around the thread several times and gently tighten the twists.

**2** Holding the thread taut, turn the needle and insert it a short distance away at 2. Keeping the thread taut, take the needle through to the back, forming a knot at 2.

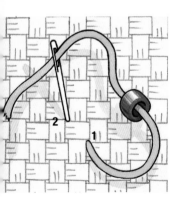

## Applying beads

Attach each bead with a half-cross stitch. Bring the needle through at 1, thread the bead, and insert the needle at 2. For a more secure fixing, make a second diagonal stitch through the bead in the same way.

### Beading tips
- Choose a suitable bead size to match the count of your fabric.
- Take care to fasten off thread ends securely to avoid the beads becoming loose and pulling away from the fabric.
- Match the thread color to that of the fabric, not the bead.
- Some highly colored beads are not colorfast, so wash and press your embroidery before applying them.

# Design tips

Here are some useful guidelines for combining multiple motifs, alphabets, and borders to design samplers and pictures.

## Combining motifs to make a sampler

To build up the design for a sampler using several motifs from the book, start by drawing your chosen motifs on graph paper. If you plan to repeat the same motif draw it out as many times as required. Cut out each graph-paper

## Adding corners to a border

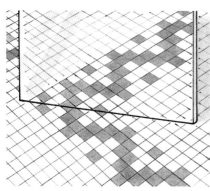

There are plenty of borders in the book that can be used just as they are, but you will probably also want to use a border pattern to make a continuous frame around a sampler, or to edge a tablecloth or decorative runner. To help you work out a good corner design from your chosen border, first draw a length of the border on graph paper and color it in. Angle a small mirror at 45 degrees to the drawn border then move the mirror until you achieve a satisfactory corner arrangement—made by the drawn border and the reflected image. Now draw the arrangement in on the graph paper.

◇ MY FAVORITE SAMPLER
TOM PUDDING DESIGNS
This large, elaborate sampler combines many pictorial and geometric motifs arranged round a central alphabet. A wide range of thread colors have been used, together with tiny seed beads and a gilt charm.

⬦ RED ALPHABETS
Tom Pudding Designs
A simple arrangement of alphabets
stitched in shades of red thread on white
fabric works well surrounded by an
antique wooden cross frame.

motif leaving a margin of one or two squares all around each one. Now spread the motifs out on a large sheet of graph paper and begin moving them around until you are happy with the arrangement, adding lettering if you wish. When using lots of small motifs try arranging them in neat rows, as if you were placing them on a chessboard. When you are happy with the arrangement stick each motif in position using double-sided tape.

## Spacing letters and numbers

As well as personalizing your own stitching by adding your name and the date of completion, you may also want to add lettering to special gifts, such as a wedding or other commemorative sampler. Write out the words you would like to use and choose one of the alphabets from the book. The height of each alphabet is given on page 253. For example, 7h means that each letter is seven crosses high when stitched. Use the same technique of drawing each letter or number on graph paper as if you were making a sampler (*see above*). Cut out the letters, leaving a one-square margin all around, then arrange them to form words. As a general guideline, space all the letters or numbers out evenly, remembering that you will need to leave a larger gap between words than you do between individual letters. For a small

alphabet, try leaving a space of a single square between letters and two squares between words. When you are happy with the spacing, double check the spelling before sticking each letter in place with double-sided tape.

## Making a key

Choose a selection of threads to stitch your design with and then color in the different motifs using fiber-tip pens or colored pencils in similar colors to the threads. For every color you use, draw and fill in a small square along the side of the chart to make a key. Write the code number of each thread by the relevant colored-in square.

## Working guidelines

Following a few simple guidelines can help you work with ease, and ensure that your embroidery stays looking fresh. Using good quality fabric and threads and taking care over your work will make the difference between a standard piece of cross stitch embroidery and a future heirloom.

• **The best you can afford** Choose the best quality fabric and threads you can afford so that your cross stitch projects will look great, and stay that way for many years.

• **Buy more than you need** When buying fabric for a project, particularly an expensive evenweave linen, don't believe you are being economical by buying exactly the amount you need to fit your design. It is far better to buy a slightly larger piece of fabric that you can trim down once the stitching is complete—if you miscalculate and the edge of the stitching finishes up too close to the fabric edge, you may not be able to use it.

• **Basting guidelines** If you are not a very experienced stitcher it can help to baste a grid of running stitches across the fabric before you begin cross stitching. On Aida fabric work rows of running stitches ten blocks apart and on evenweave fabric work them twenty threads apart. This divides the fabric into ten-stitch blocks that make following a chart easier.

• **Work outward** Start stitching at the center of the design and work outward so that you have an even margin of fabric all around the stitched design.

• **Work cleanly** Nothing spoils a piece of cross stitch more than grubby fingerprints or a dirty ring where the fabric has been rubbed around an embroidery hoop. Always wash your hands thoroughly before starting to stitch and at regular intervals during your stitching session, and avoid using hand cream when you are stitching because the oils in the cream may transfer to the fabric. It is also good practice to take an embroidery out of its hoop at the end of each stitching session.

• **Avoid fluff** Try to avoid wearing dark-colored garments that shed while you are stitching—angora or mohair jumpers are the worst because the tiny hairs they shed get trapped beneath the stitches. If fluff accumulates on your work clean it off by wrapping adhesive tape around your hand, sticky side out, and gently dabbing it over the surface of the stitching.

• **Care for work in progress** Store threads and unfinished work in a clean, dark, and dry place. An old, well-washed cotton pillowcase is ideal for this, but if you decide to use a paper bag or embroidery tote bag for temporary storage, protect your work from dirt by wrapping it in white, acid-free tissue paper first. Store leftover threads carefully. You can buy precut card bobbins to wind the threads round, or cut out your own from a sheet of thin card. Make a note of the brand and color number of the thread on each card, place the cards in a dustproof box, then store in a cool, dry place.

# Looking after your completed work

When your stitching is complete, give some thought to how best to look after it, so that you and your family can enjoy the fruits of your labor for many years to come.

## Washing guidelines

Make it a cast-iron rule to treat spills and stains as soon as they occur and mend tears or holes before laundering. If you are worried that the threads used in a piece may not be colorfast, have the item dry cleaned.

Embroidered items such as table linen and pillowcases that are intended to be used rather than displayed will need to be laundered. The best way to do this is to wash the items carefully by hand in hand-hot water with a mild, detergent-free cleaning agent. Most specialist fabric shampoos are ideal, but check that the one you choose does not contain optical brighteners, which will cause colors to fade.

Rinse the piece thoroughly in several changes of water, then roll it in a towel and press gently to remove surplus water. Gently ease the embroidery into shape and leave to dry out of direct sunlight.

## Pressing guidelines

Press embroidered pieces while they are still slightly damp. Pad the ironing surface with a couple of old, clean towels then lay the embroidery over them with the wrong side uppermost. Cover with a piece of clean white fabric—an old cotton sheet is perfect. Set the iron to a temperature that matches the

composition of the fabric: linen setting for evenweave linen; slightly cooler for Aida and cotton fabrics; and a lower synthetic setting for fabric made from a cotton/synthetic blend. Press lightly, taking care not to flatten the stitches.

## Storage

Frame pictures to eliminate dust and dirt and store items such as table and bed linen carefully when not in use.

The main enemies that can attack embroideries, apart from dust and dirt, are direct sunlight and strong artificial lighting, which cause colors to fade and fibers to weaken. Heat makes both the threads and fabric brittle, while damp rots the fibers, so display framed pieces carefully, avoiding positions close to fireplaces and radiators and rooms with humid atmospheres, such as bathrooms.

Try not to store fabric items for any length of time in polythene bags because the polythene

attracts dirt and dust that will transfer readily to the fabric. Polythene also prevents natural fibers such as cotton and linen from breathing, causing them to weaken and eventually rot, and can result in mildew attacks. Instead, store small items flat and larger ones rolled around an acid-free card tube protected by layers of white acid-free tissue paper. Items that are too large to roll should be loosely folded between layers of white acid-free tissue paper, making sure each fold is padded with more tissue

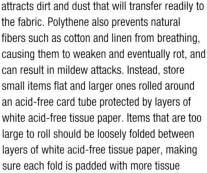

paper. Store all the items in their own, clean, fabric bag in a drawer, cupboard, or other dark, dry, and moth-free place.

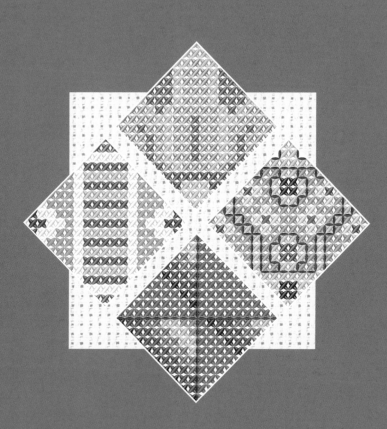

# Chapter

# Pattern Library

The Pattern Library contains charts for over 1000 cross stitch motifs, divided into eleven different themes for ease of use. Each page is accompanied by a key showing the colors used. Details of motif sizes and thread numbers are given at the end of the library.

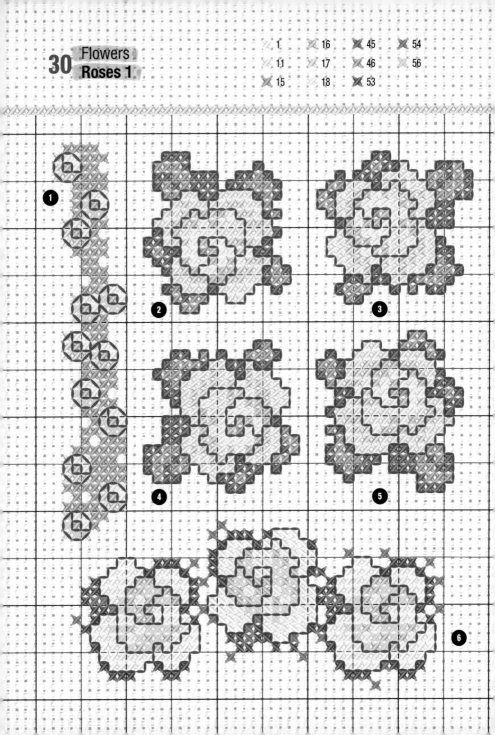

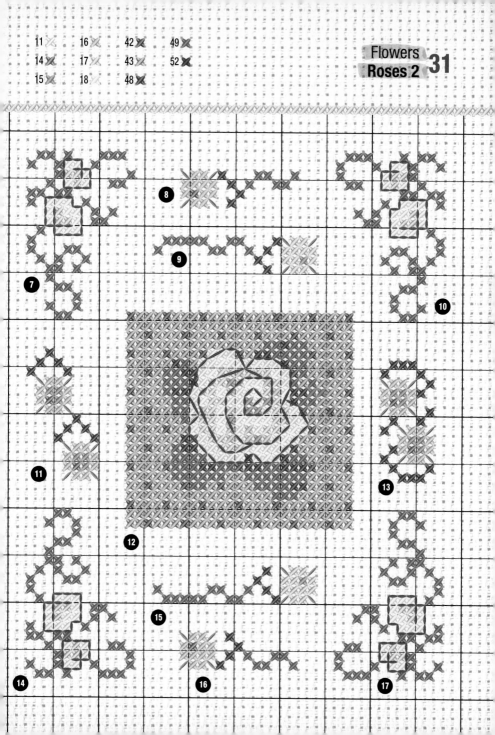

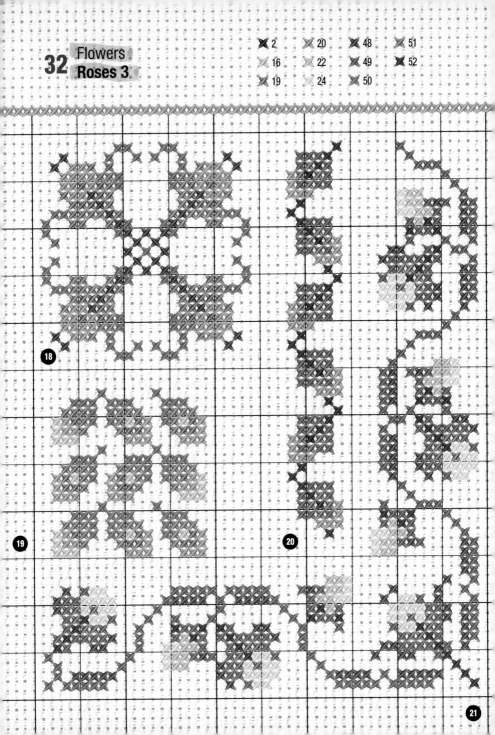

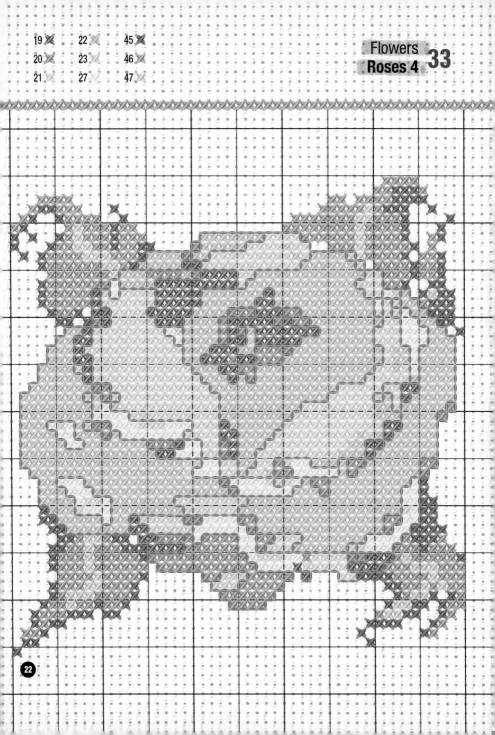

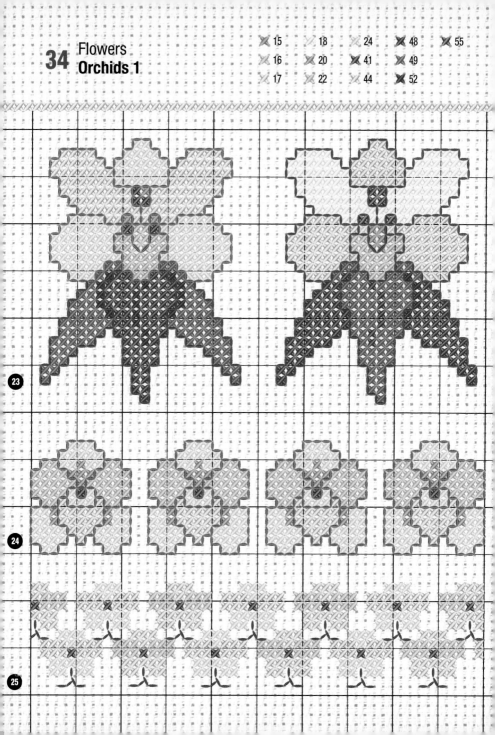

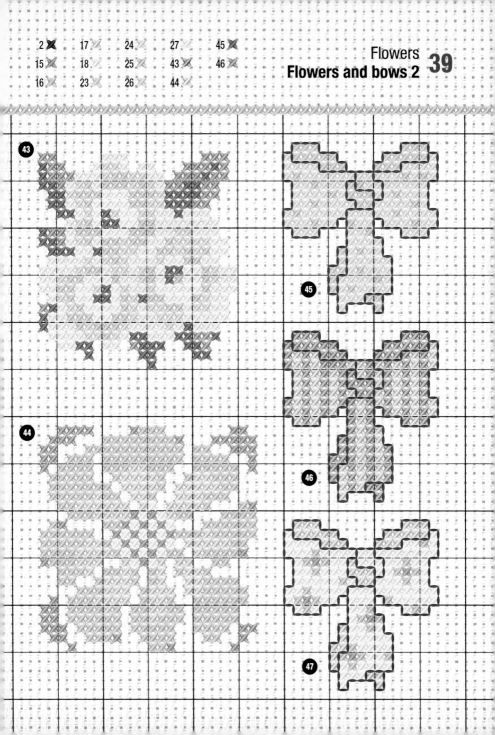

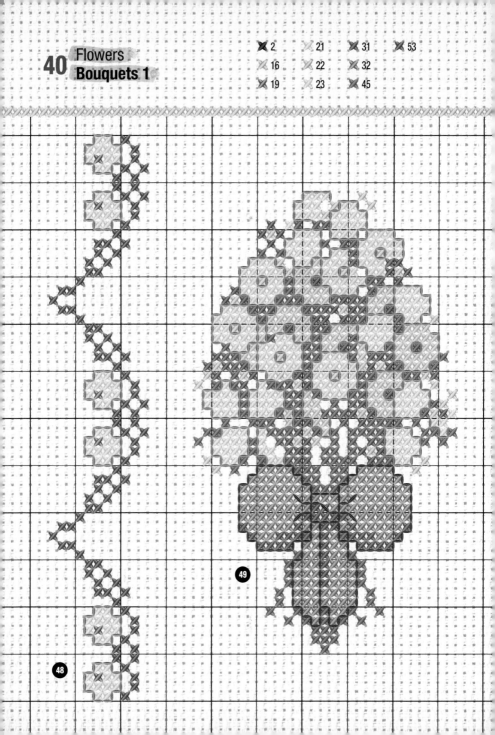

| ✖ 2 | ✖ 21 | ✖ 31 | ✖ 53 |
| ✖ 16 | ✖ 22 | ✖ 32 | |
| ✖ 19 | ✖ 23 | ✖ 45 | |

49

48

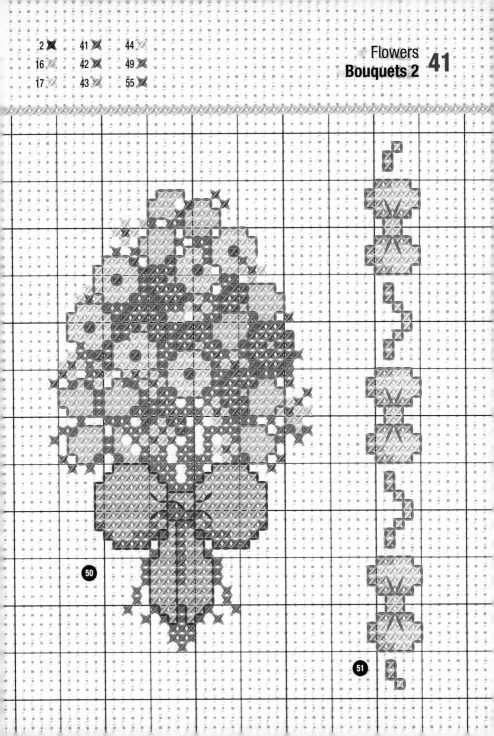

## 42 Flowers
### Flower motifs 1

| | | |
|---|---|---|
| ✕ 14 | ✕ 17 | ✕ 49 |
| ✕ 15 | ✕ 45 | ✕ 52 |
| ✕ 16 | ✕ 46 | ✕ 55 |

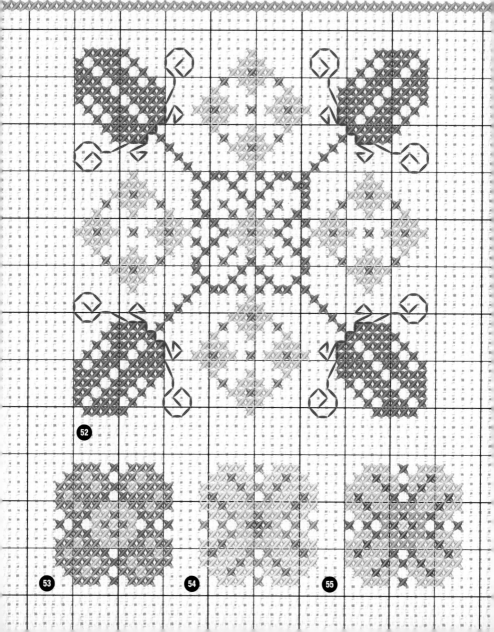

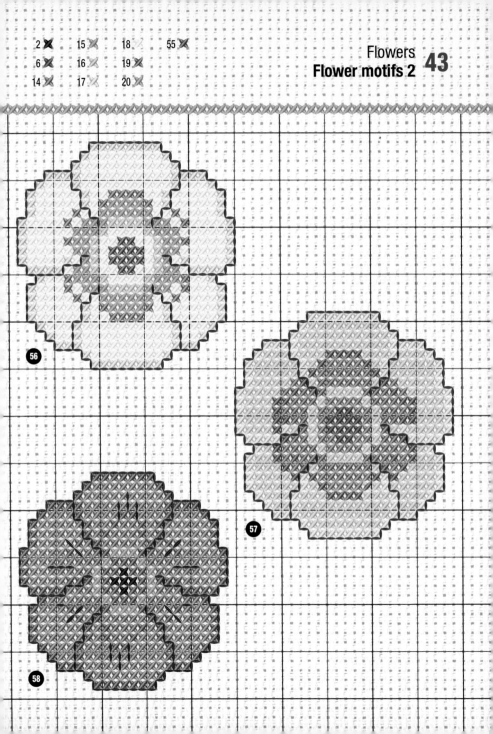

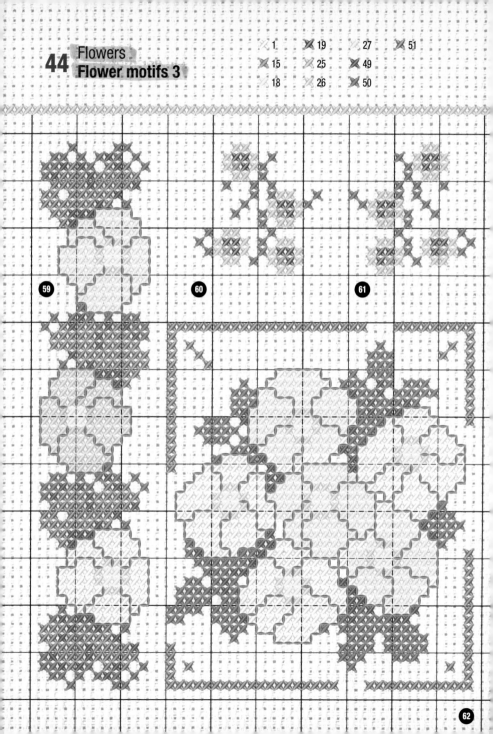

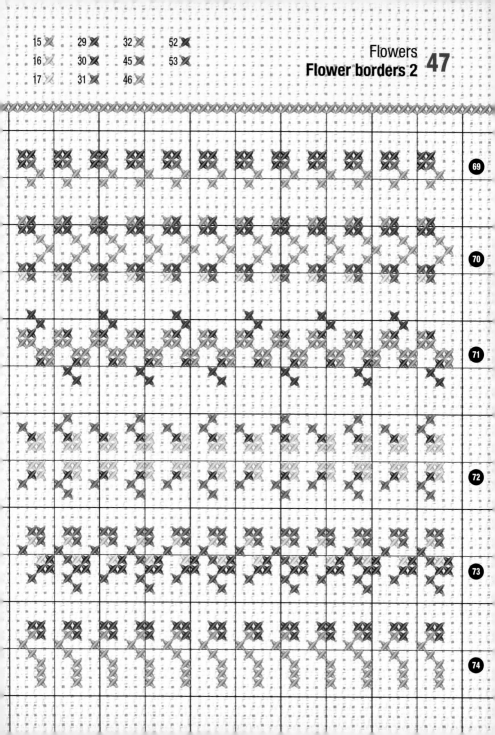

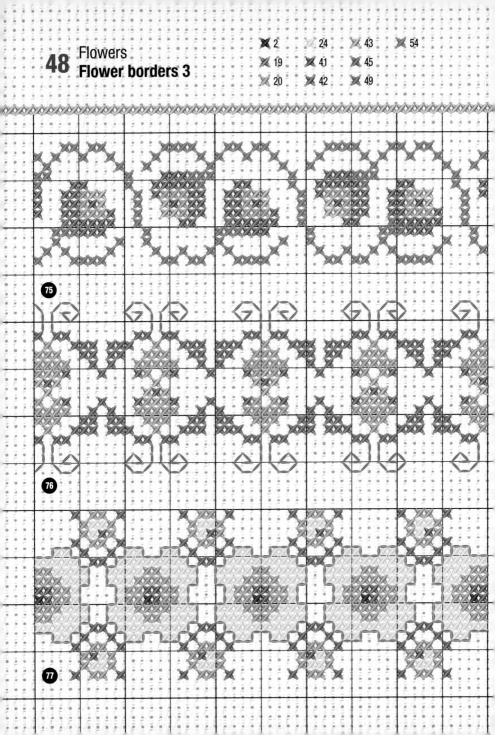

**Flowers**

# 48 Flower borders 3

Legend:
- ✖ 2
- ✖ 19
- ✖ 20
- ✖ 24
- ✖ 41
- ✖ 42
- ✖ 43
- ✖ 45
- ✖ 49
- ✖ 54

75

76

77

2 ✖  42 ✖  49 ✖
22 ✖  43 ✖  50 ✖
31 ✖  44 ✖  52 ✖

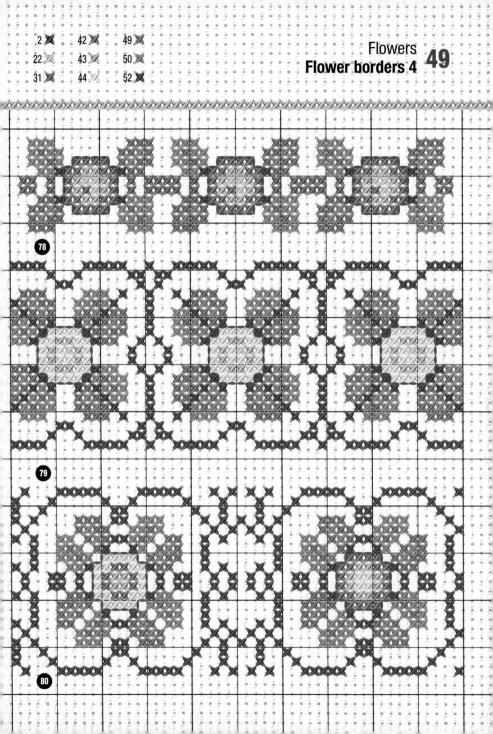

# Home and garden
## Country garden 1

| | | | | |
|---|---|---|---|---|
| 2 | 20 | 27 | 33 | 51 |
| 13 | 23 | 28 | 45 | 52 |
| 19 | 24 | 31 | 46 | |

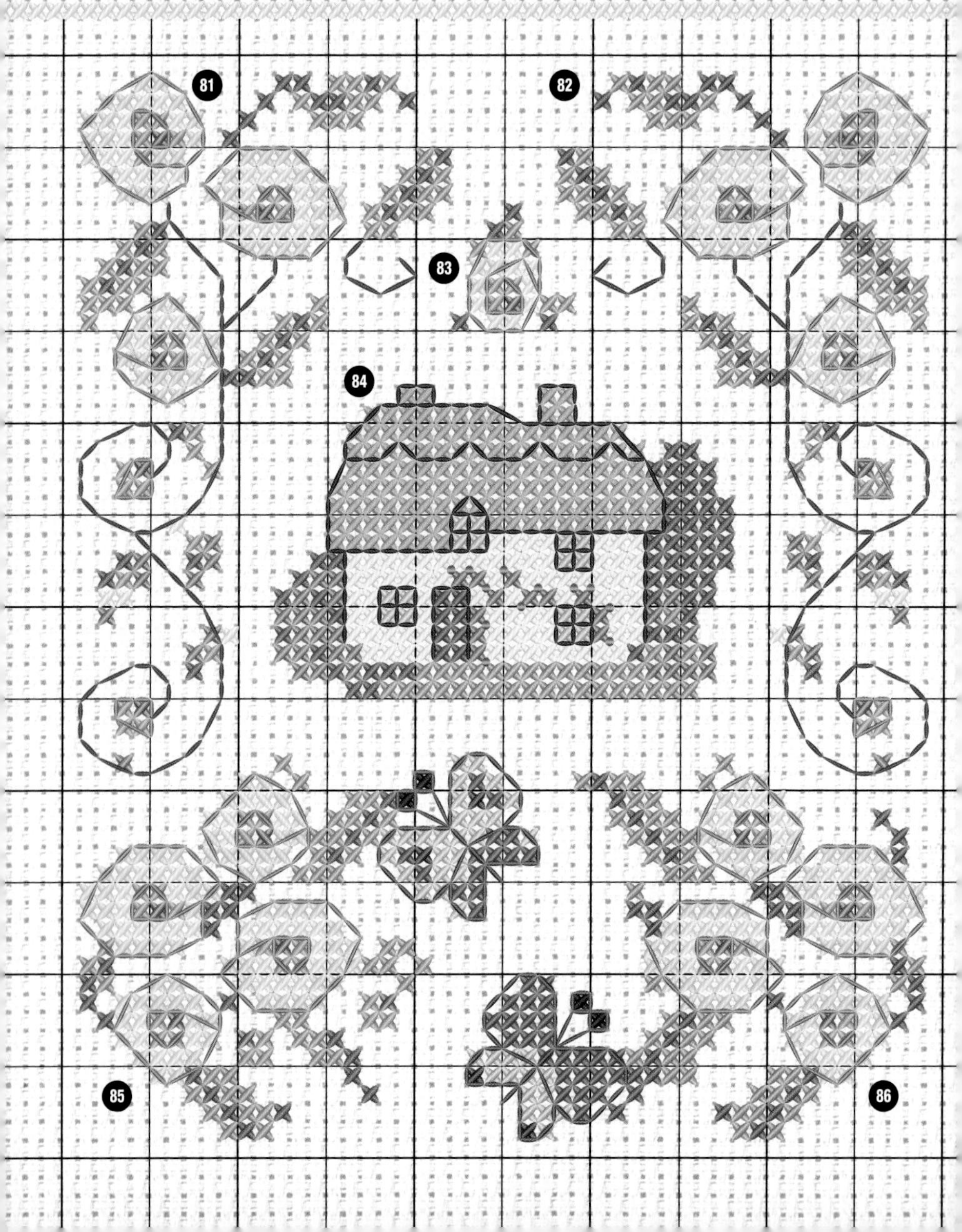

1   12   17   23   46
2   13   19   24   52
11   16   20   45

| | | | | |
|---|---|---|---|---|
| ⊠ 1 | ⊠ 5 | ⊠ 12 | ⊠ 19 | ⊠ 50 |
| ⊠ 2 | ⊠ 7 | ⊠ 13 | ⊠ 20 | ⊠ 51 |
| ⊠ 4 | ⊠ 11 | ⊠ 14 | ⊠ 42 | |

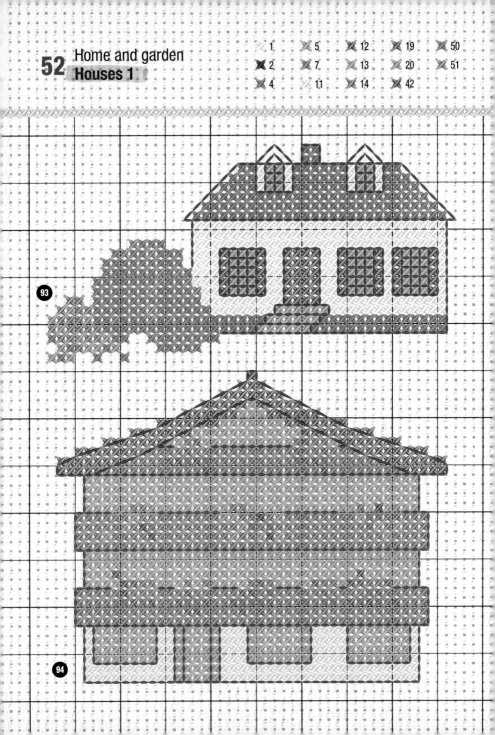

93

94

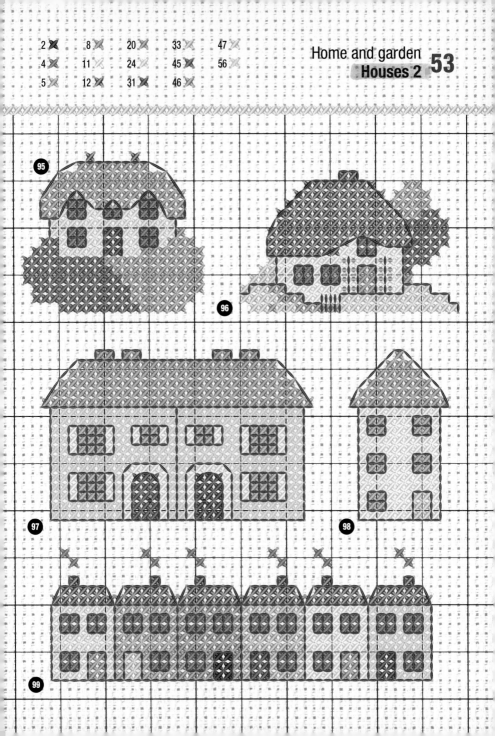

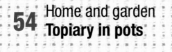

✖ 6  ✖ 46  ✖ 56
✖ 13  ✖ 47  ✖ 57
✖ 45  ✖ 52

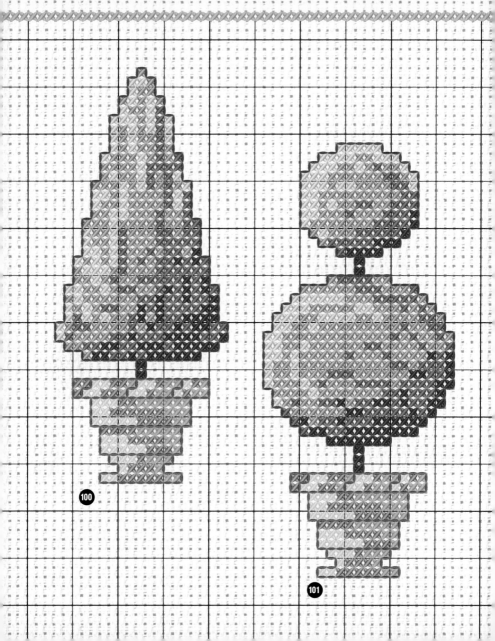

**100**

**101**

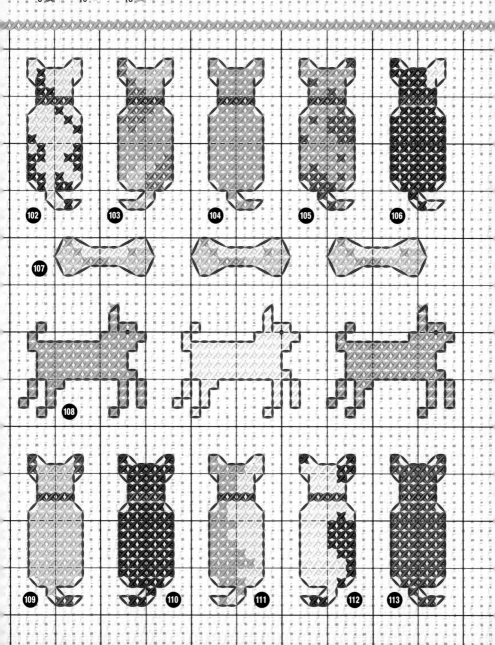

Key:
- 1
- 2
- 4
- 7
- 8
- 11
- 12
- 13
- 14
- 24
- 32
- 34
- 50

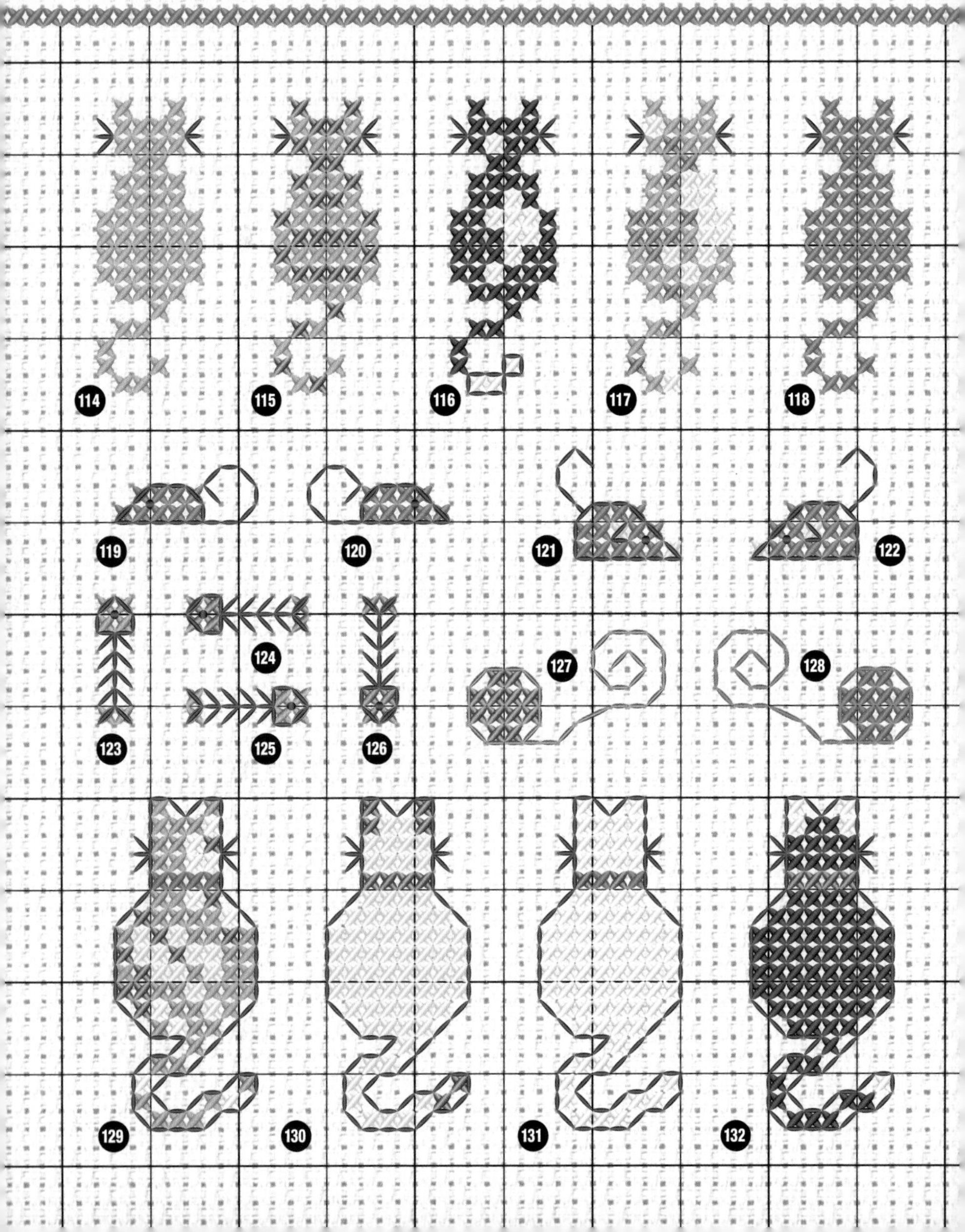

114  115  116  117  118

119  120  121  122

123  124  125  126  127  128

129  130  131  132

1   5   12   31
2   8   13   50
4   11   15

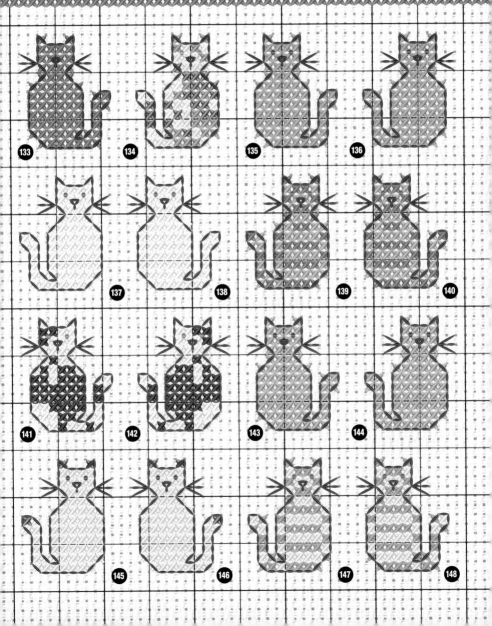

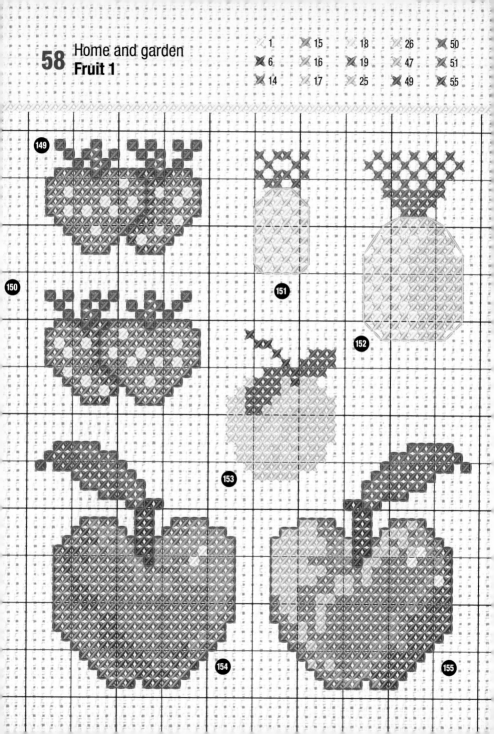

# 58 Home and garden
## Fruit 1

× 1  × 15  × 18  × 26  × 50
× 6  × 16  × 19  × 47  × 51
× 14  × 17  × 25  × 49  × 55

149
150
151
152
153
154
155

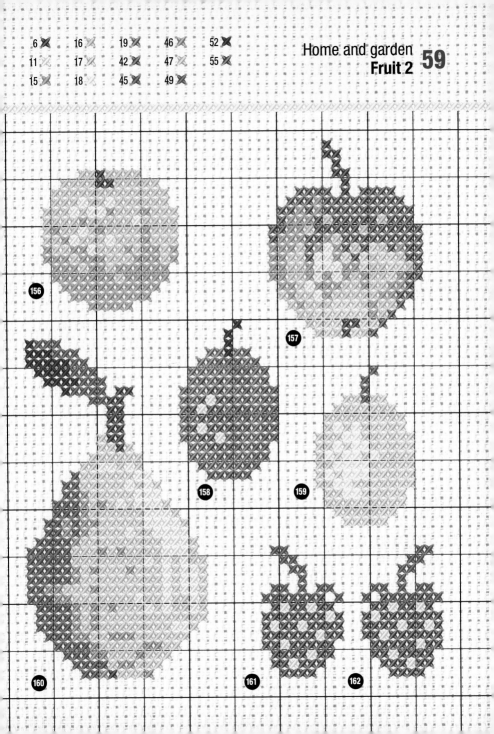

| | | | | | |
|---|---|---|---|---|---|
| ╳ 1 | ╳ 13 | ╳ 21 | ╳ 33 | ╳ 46 | |
| ╳ 2 | ╳ 19 | ╳ 29 | ╳ 41 | ╳ 48 | |
| ╳ 12 | ╳ 20 | ╳ 32 | ╳ 43 | ╳ 50 | |

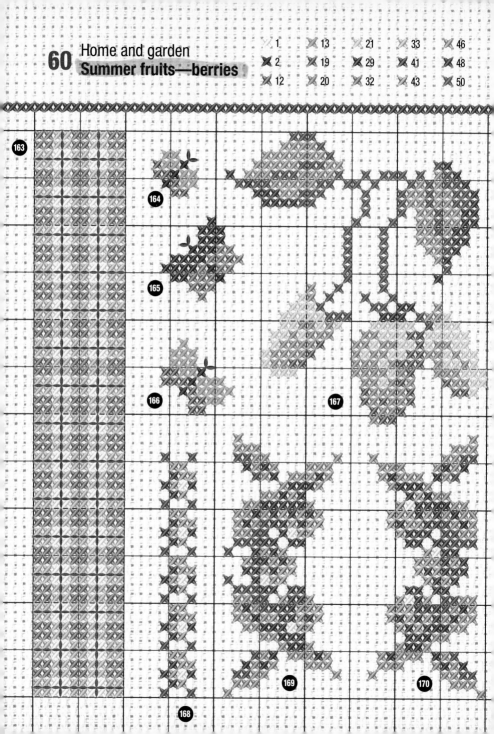

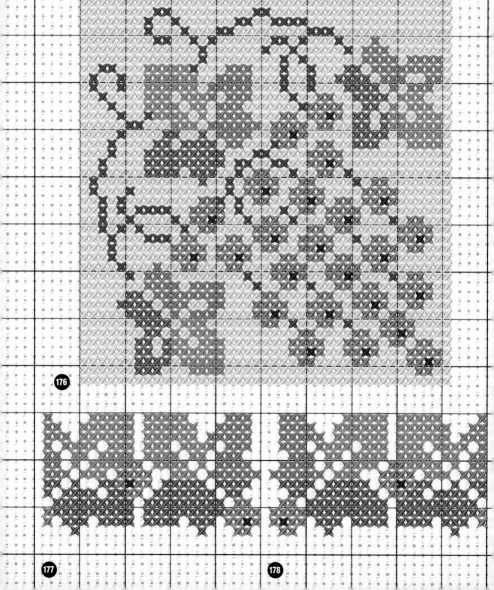

# 62 Home and garden
## Grapes 1

✕ 2    ✕ 48    ✕ 52
✕ 38   ✕ 49
✕ 42   ✕ 50

176

177        178

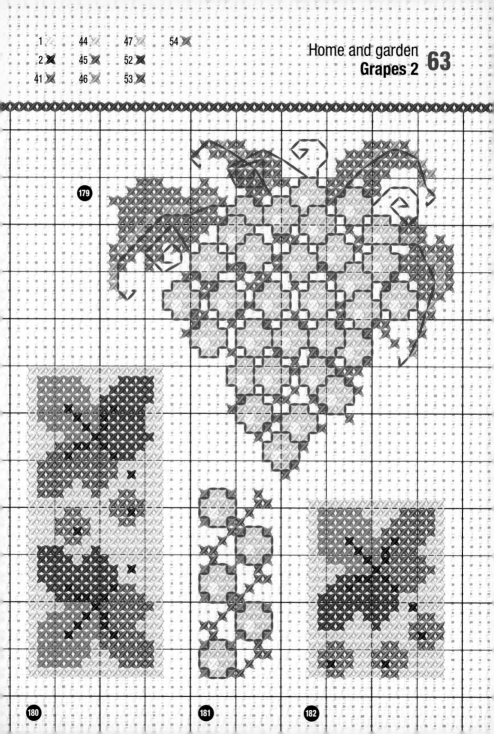

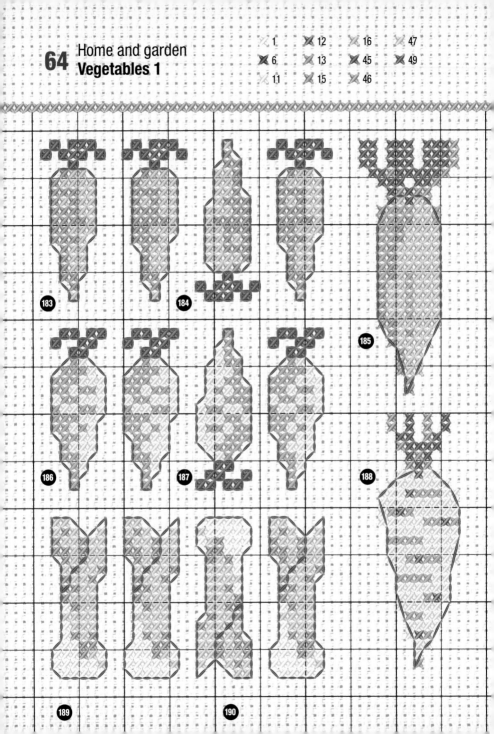

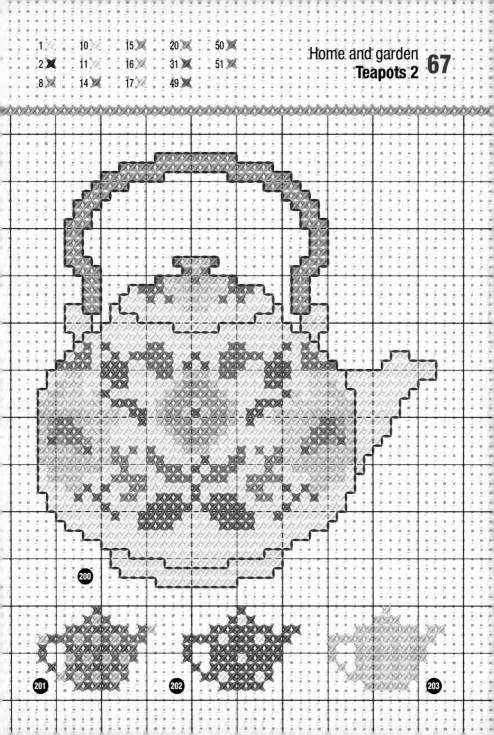

| | | | |
|---|---|---|---|
| ⊠ 1 | ✖ 4 | ✖ 15 | ✖ 55 |
| ✖ 2 | ✖ 5 | ✖ 16 | |
| ⊠ 3 | ✖ 14 | ✖ 17 | |

204

205

206

207

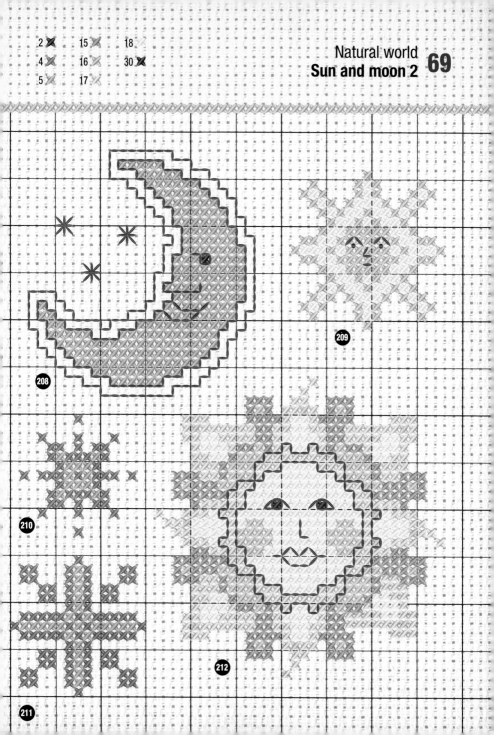

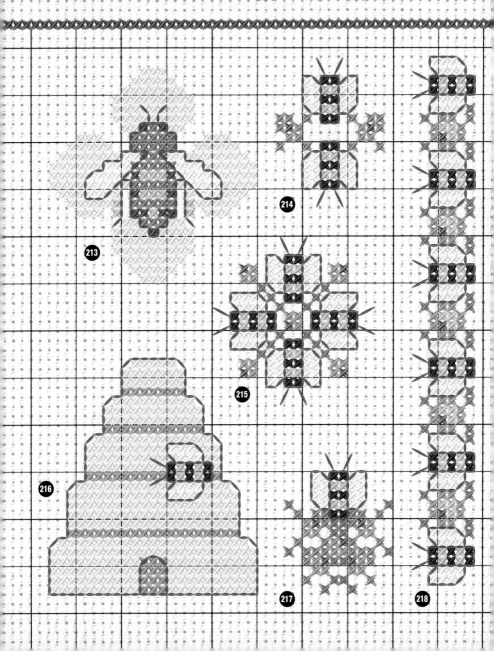

2 ✖  12 ✖  17 ✖  29 ✖  36 ✖
6 ✖  15 ✖  18 ✖  31 ✖  52 ✖
8 ✖  16 ✖  19 ✖  32 ✖

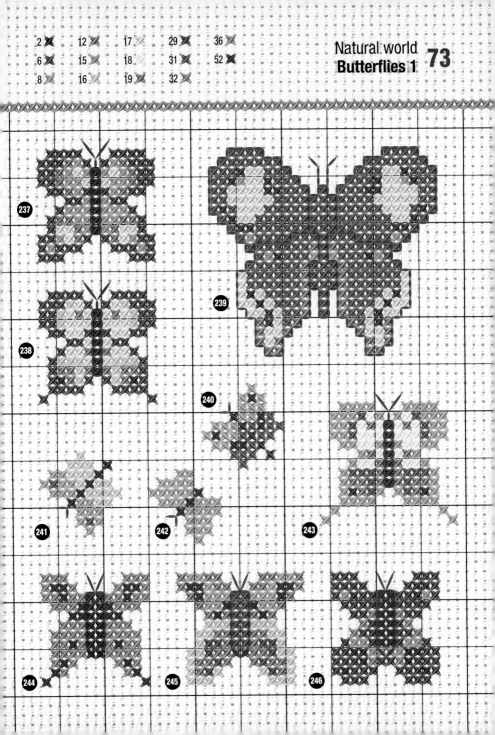

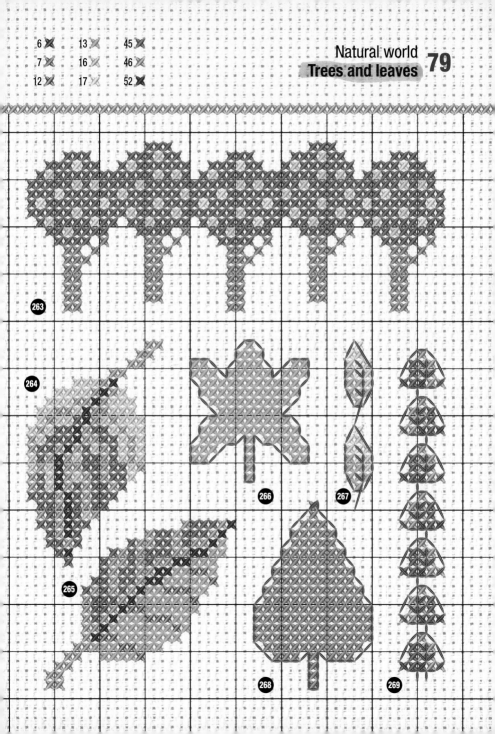

✕ 2    ✕ 7    ✕ 12    ✕ 46
✕ 4    ✕ 8    ✕ 13    ✕ 47
✕ 5    ✕ 9    ✕ 45

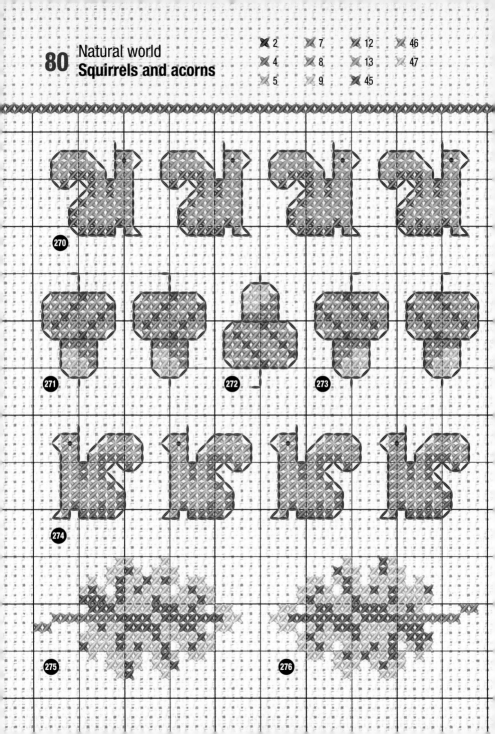

270
271
272
273
274
275
276

2 ✕   12 ✕
8 ✕   45 ✕
9 ✕   47 ✕

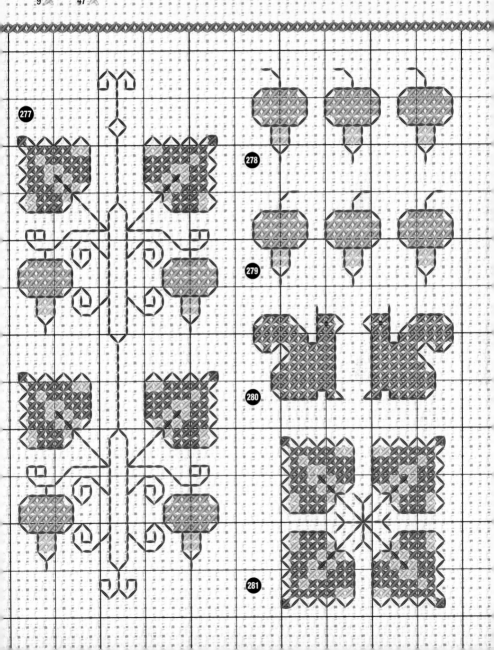

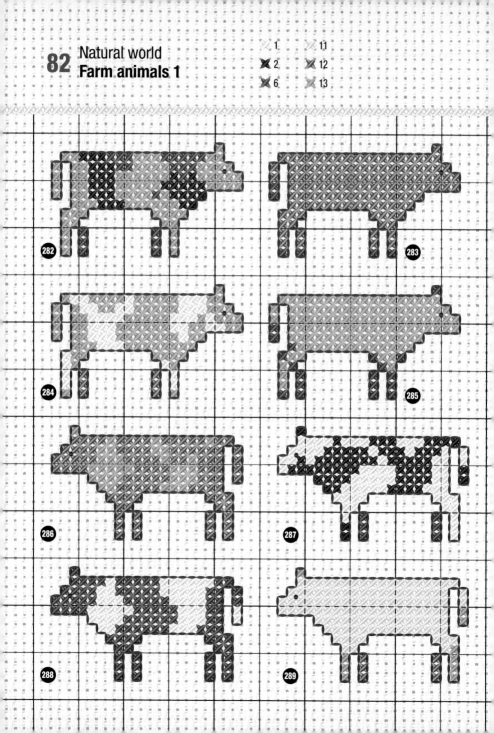

2 ✖  17 ✖  40 ✖  52 ✖
14 ✖  18 ✖  50 ✖  55 ✖
16 ✖  32 ✖  51 ✖

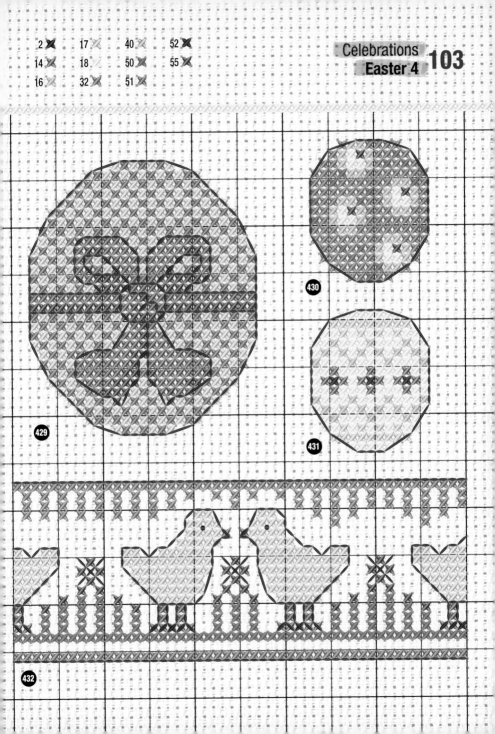

429

430

431

432

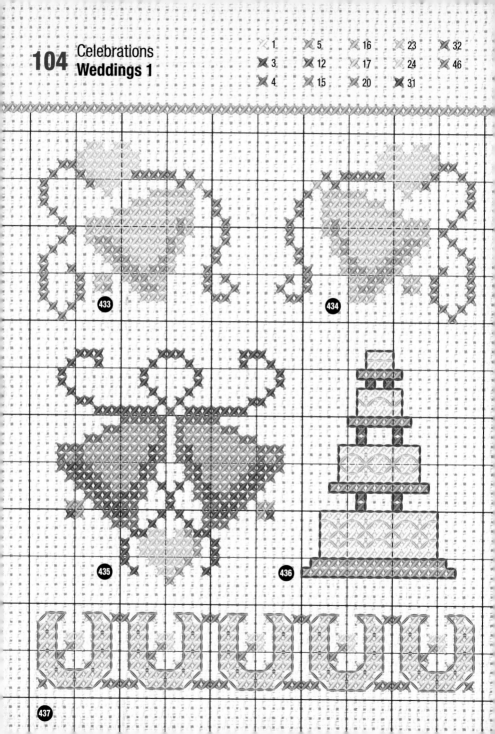

1   4   11   31   55

2   5   17   32

3   8   20   48

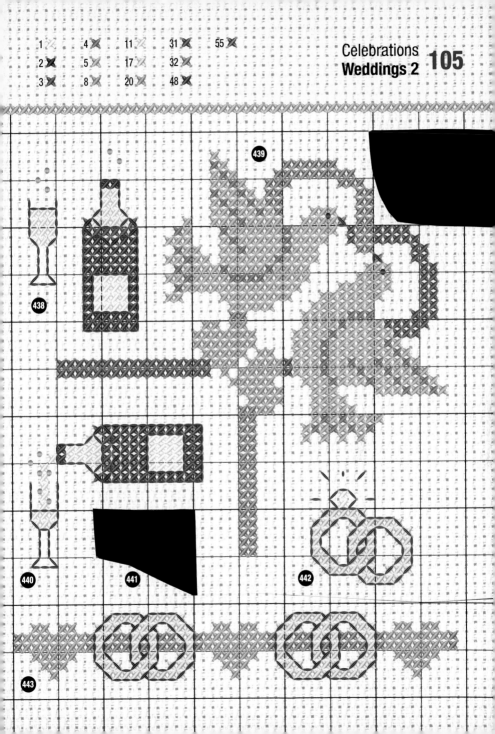

439

438

440   441   442

443

✖ 3  ✖ 42
✖ 28  ✖ 43
✖ 33  ✖ 44

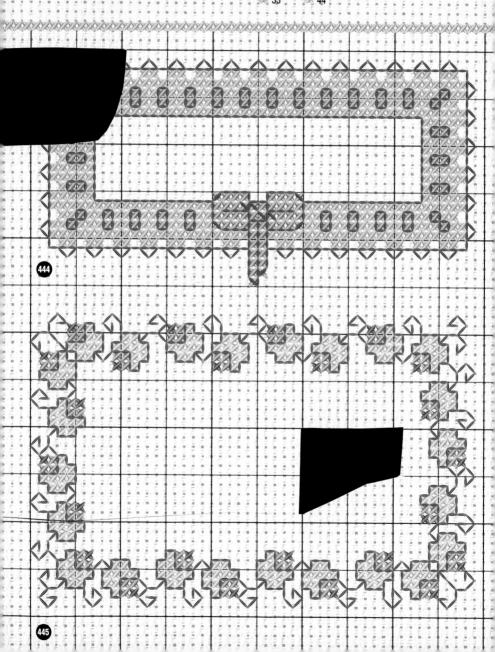

444

445

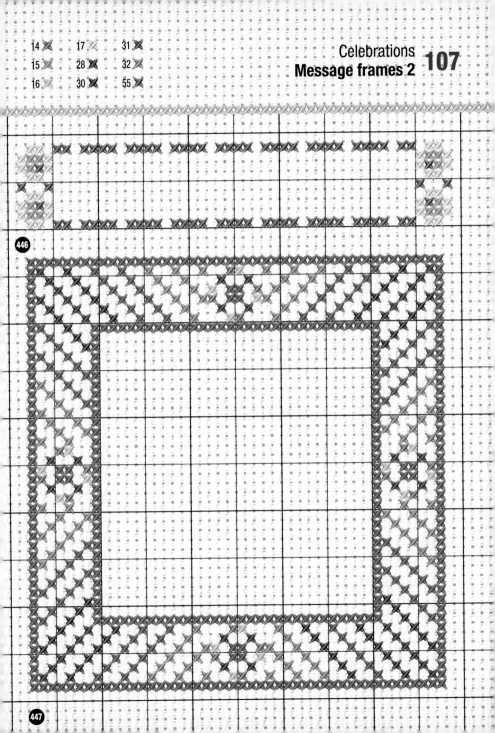

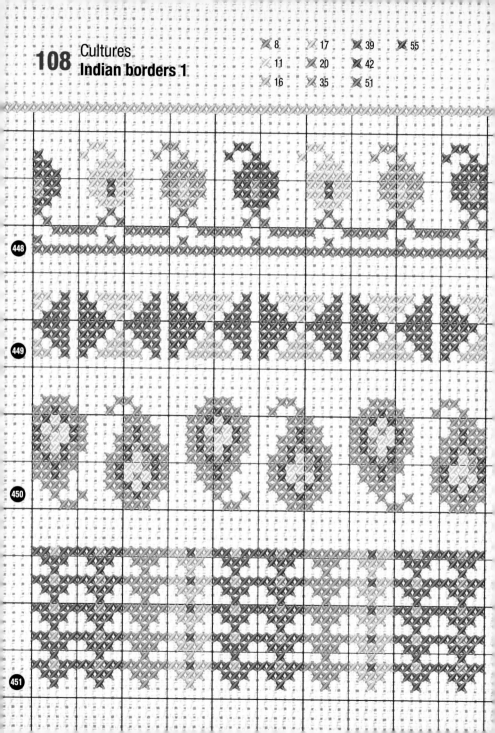

2 ✕  17 ✕  34 ✕  40 ✕
15 ✕  19 ✕  35 ✕  51 ✕
16 ✕  20 ✕  39 ✕

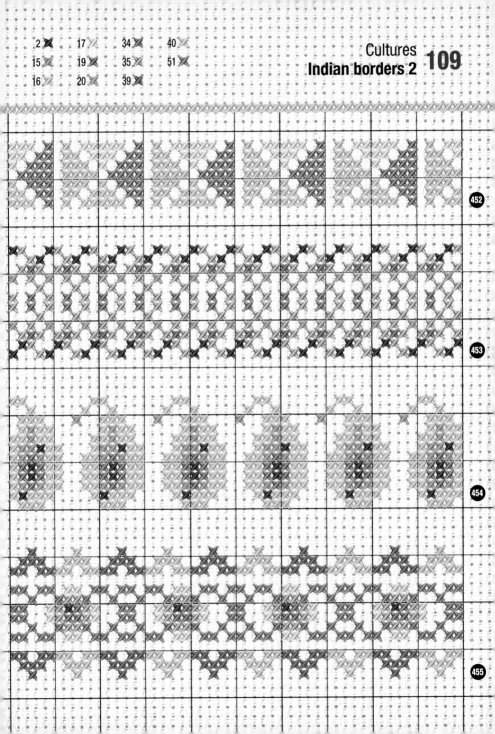

452

453

454

455

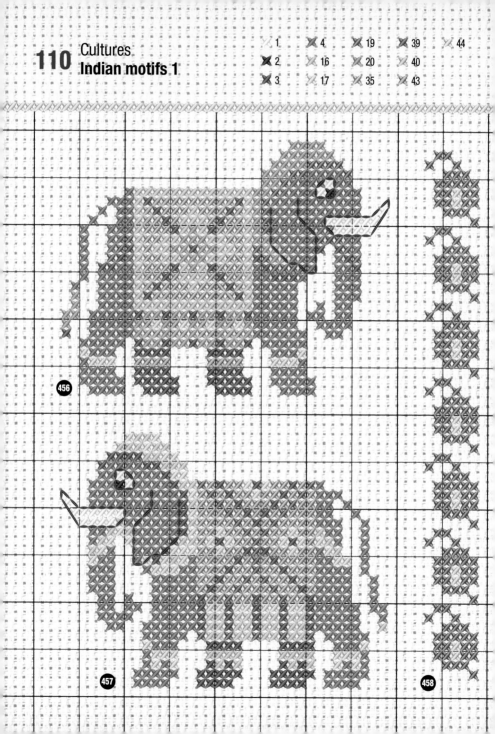

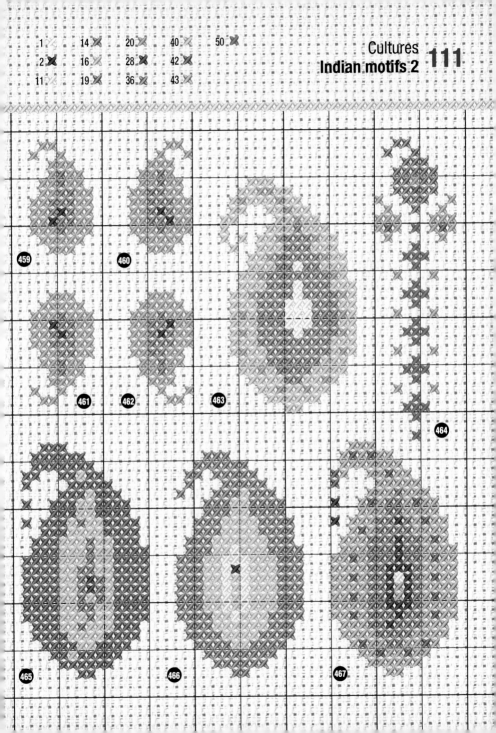

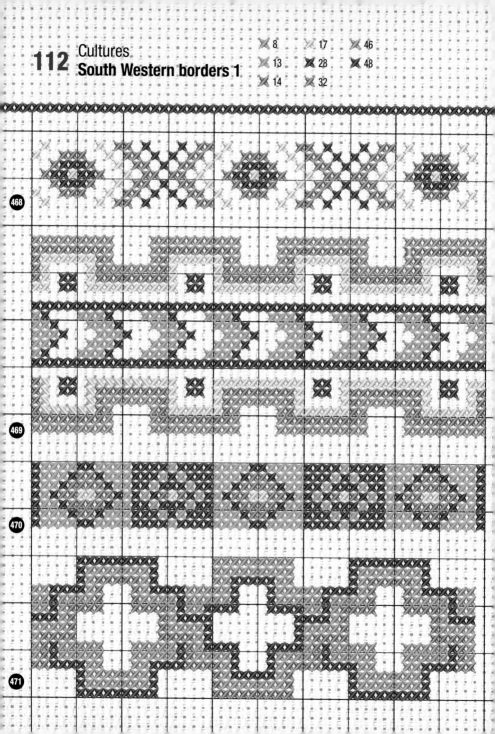

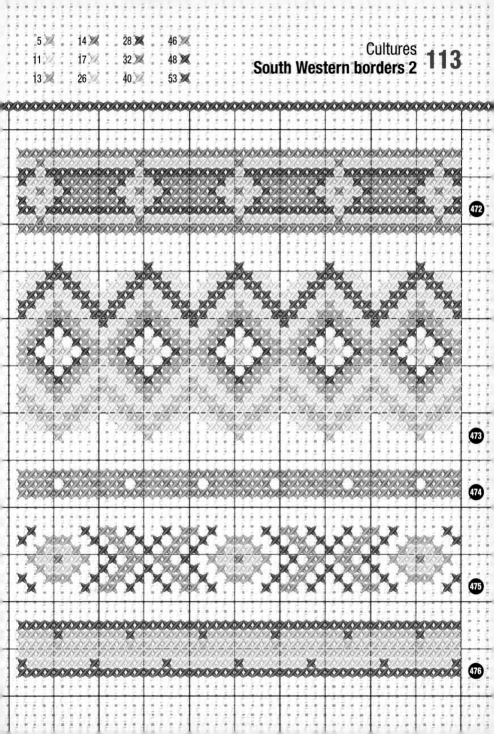

5 ☒  14 ☒  28 ☒  46 ☒
11 ☒  17 ☒  32 ☒  48 ☒
13 ☒  26 ☒  40 ☒  53 ☒

472

473

474

475

476

✕ 13  ✕ 17  ✕ 52
✕ 14  ✕ 30
✕ 16  ✕ 50

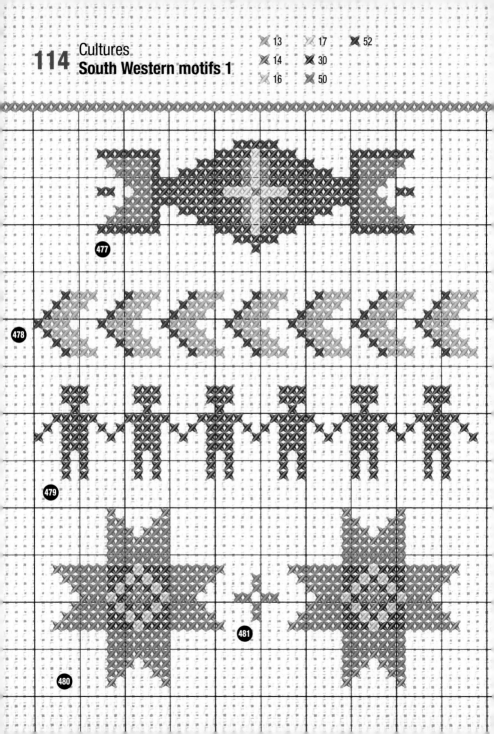

477

478

479

481

480

2 ✖   16 ✖   35 ✖
12 ✖   17 ✖   50 ✖
14 ✖   30 ✖   52 ✖

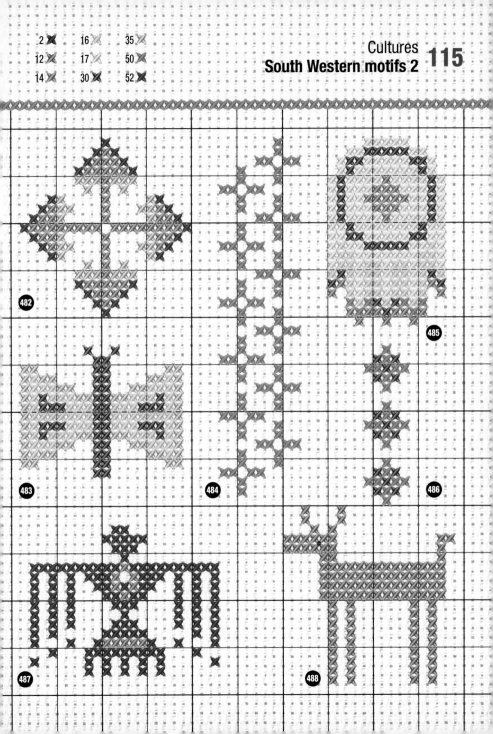

482

483

484

485

486

487

488

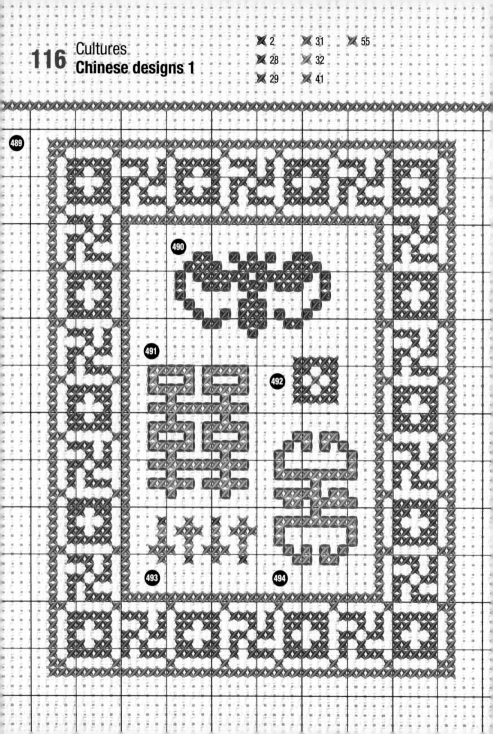

2 ✖  30 ✖
15 ✖  32 ✖
28 ✖  33 ✖

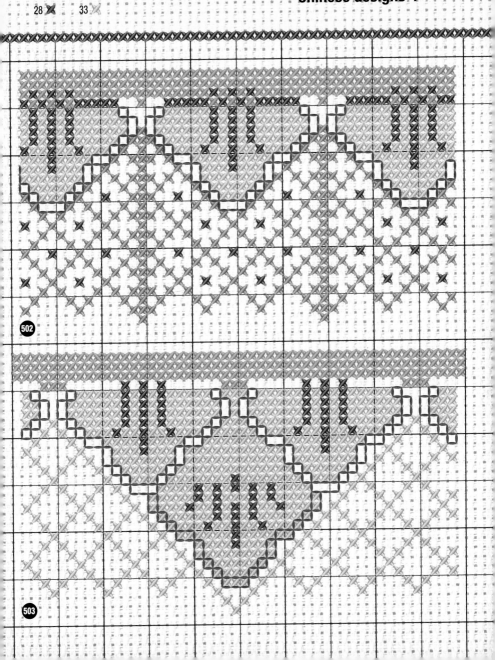

502

503

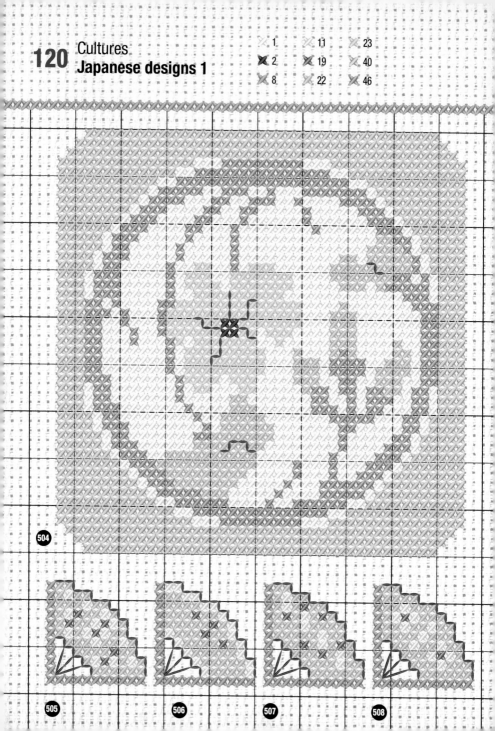

1 · 6 × 15 × 35 ×
2 × 8 × 16 × 39 ×
3 × 10 × 19 × 40 ×

517

518

519

✕ 2   ✕ 8   ✕ 16   ✕ 56
✕ 3   ✕ 9   ✕ 19   ✕ 57
✕ 6   ✕ 13   ✕ 25

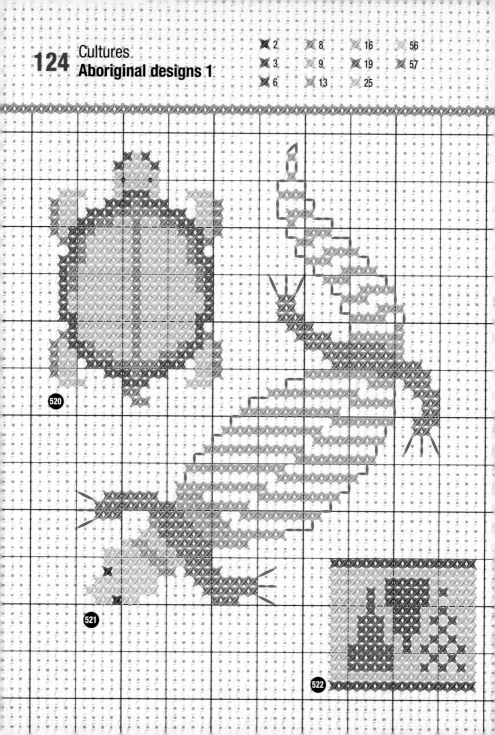

2 ✖   8 ✖   16 ✖   57 ✖
3 ✖   13 ✖   19 ✖
6 ✖   15 ✖   39 ✖

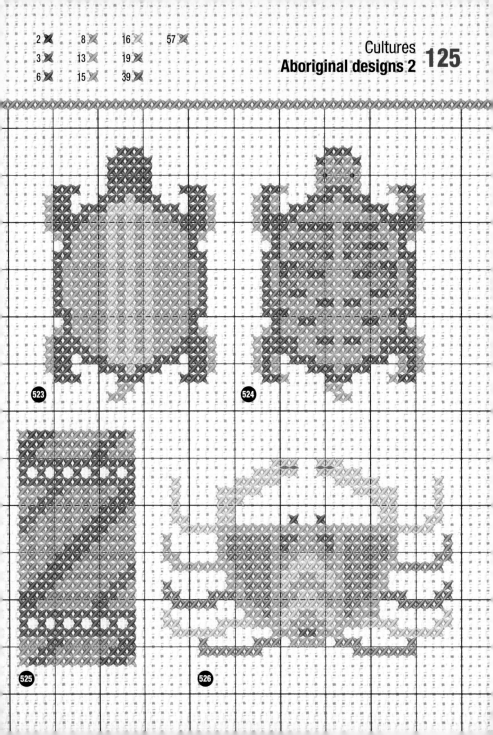

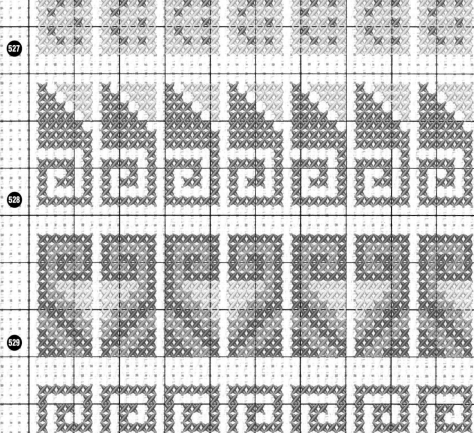

527

528

529

530

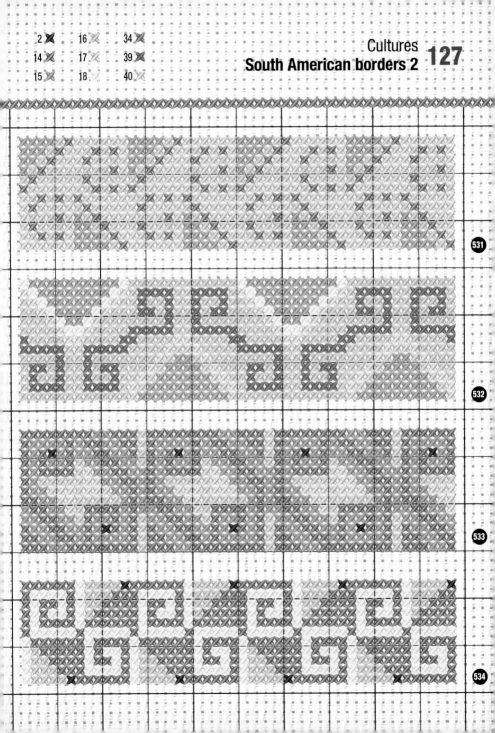

✕ 2    ✕ 35    ✕ 55
✕ 16   ✕ 40
✕ 34   ✕ 50

535

536

537

538

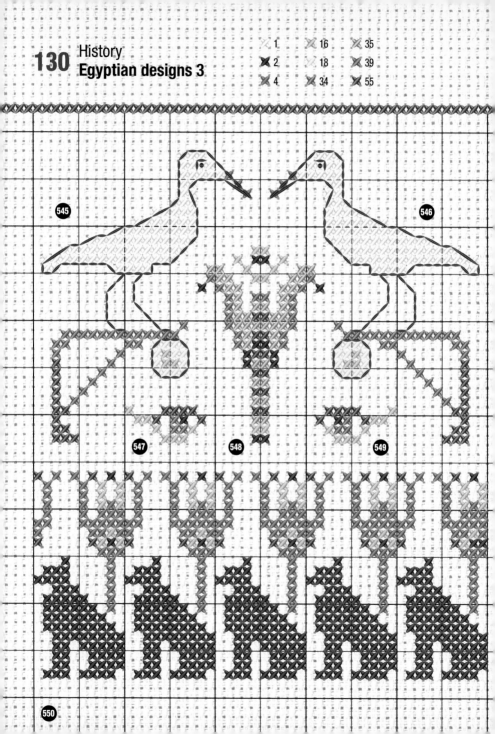

1 🖊    11 🖊    16 🖊    30 ✖
2 ✖    13 🖊    17 🖊    50 ✖
10 🖊    15 ✖    20 ✖    55 ✖

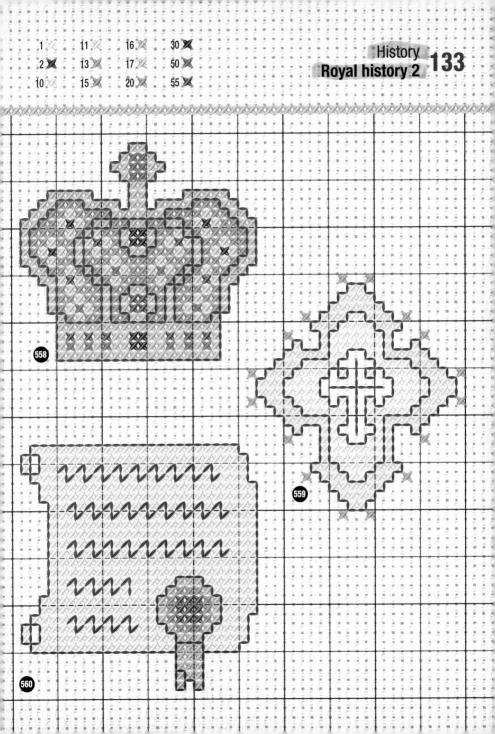

558

559

560

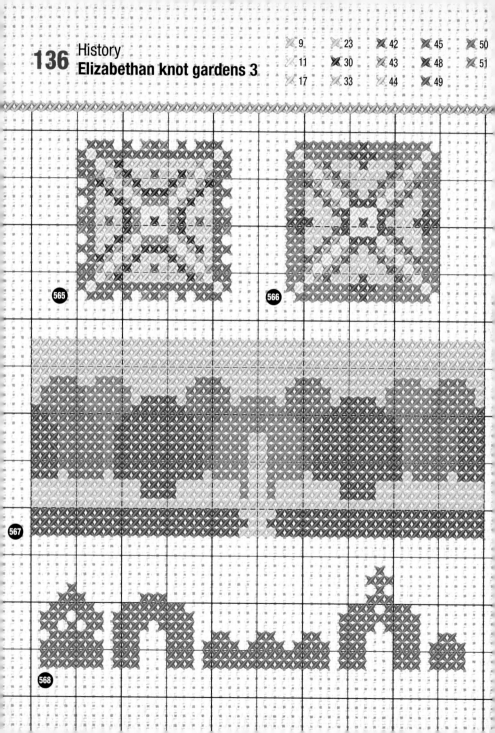

11 ✗  19 ✗  43 ✗  51 ✗
14 ✗  20 ✗  45 ✗  52 ✗
18 ✗  41 ✗  49 ✗

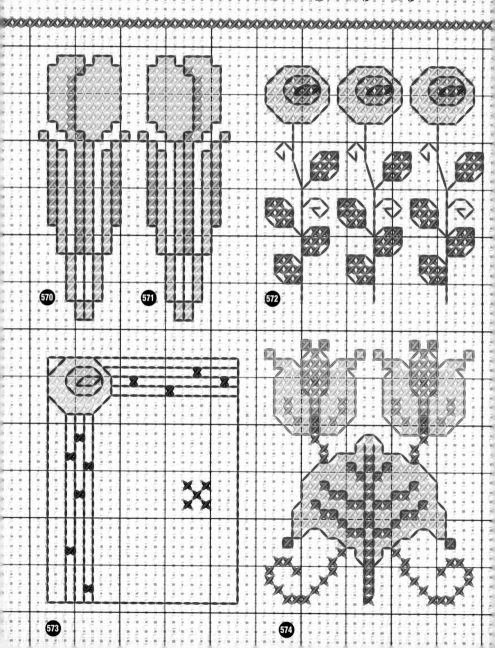

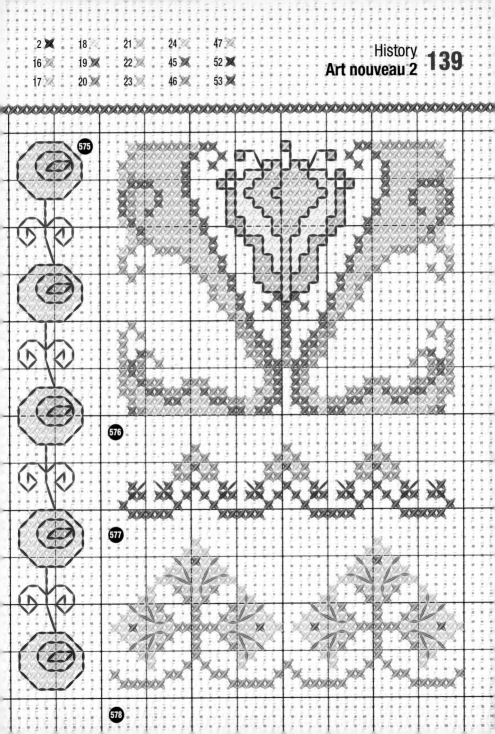

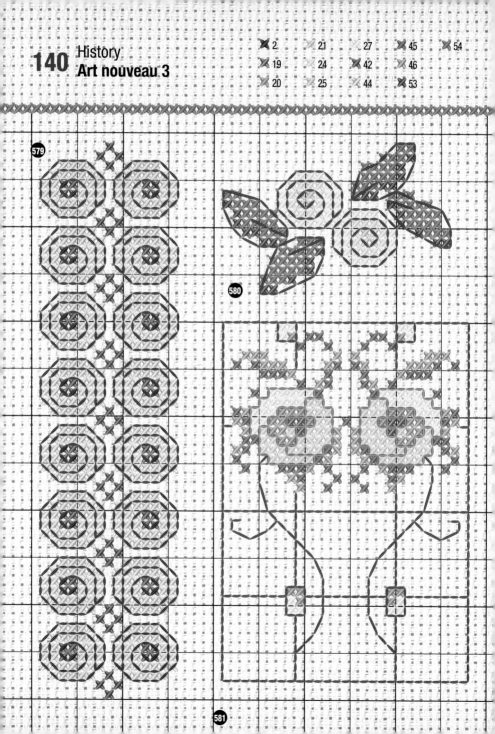

11  17  21  51  54
15  19  26  52
16  20  47  53

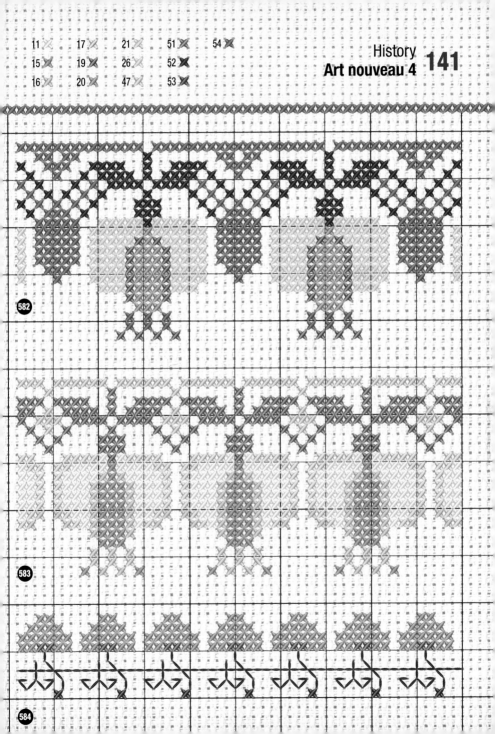

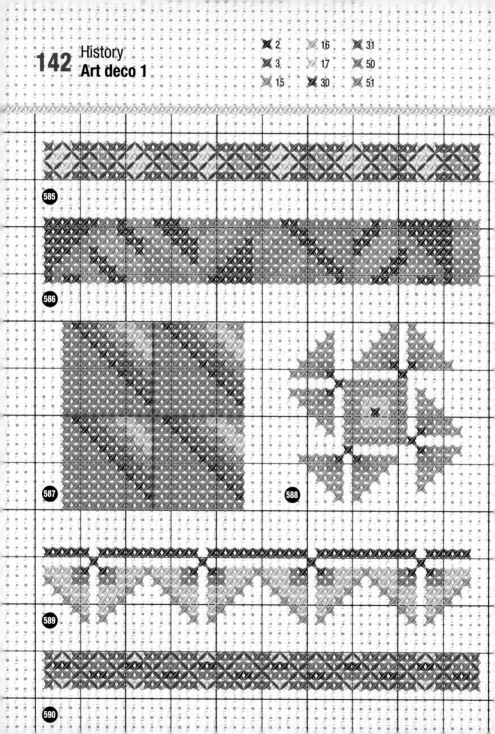

| | | |
|---|---|---|
| ✖ 2 | ✖ 16 | ✖ 31 |
| ✖ 3 | ✖ 17 | ✖ 50 |
| ✖ 15 | ✖ 30 | ✖ 51 |

585

586

587

588

589

590

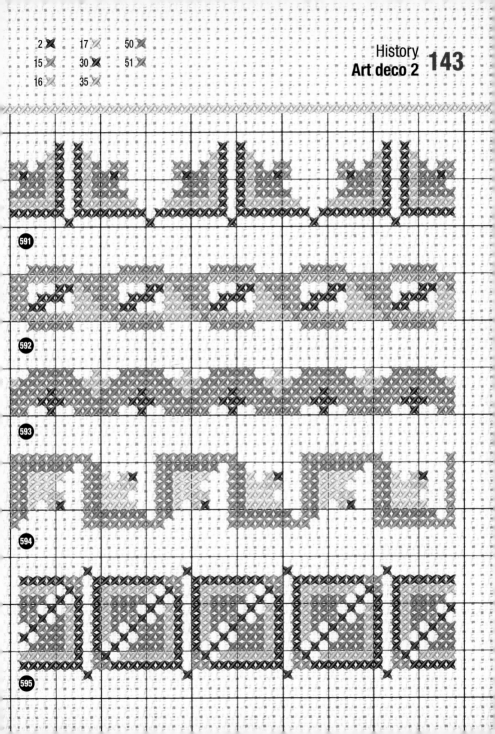

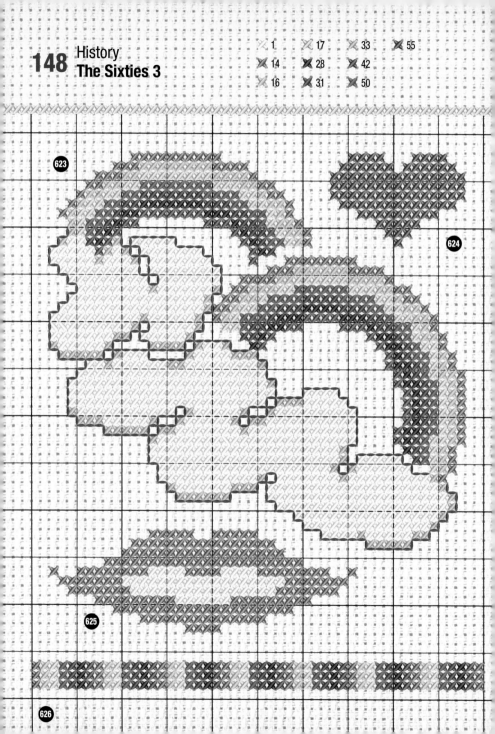

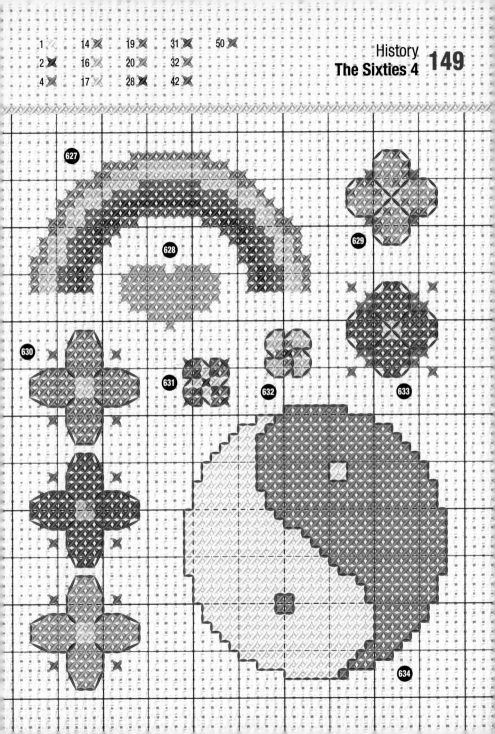

1   14   19   31   50

2   16   20   32

4   17   28   42

1 16 27 55
2 11 18 31
5 12 26 35
13

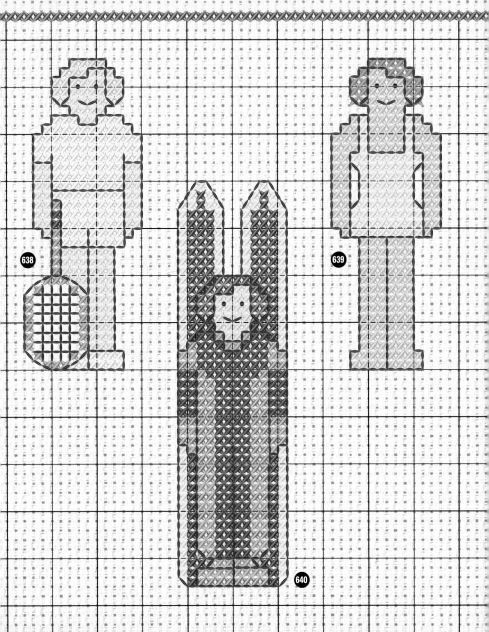

638
639
640

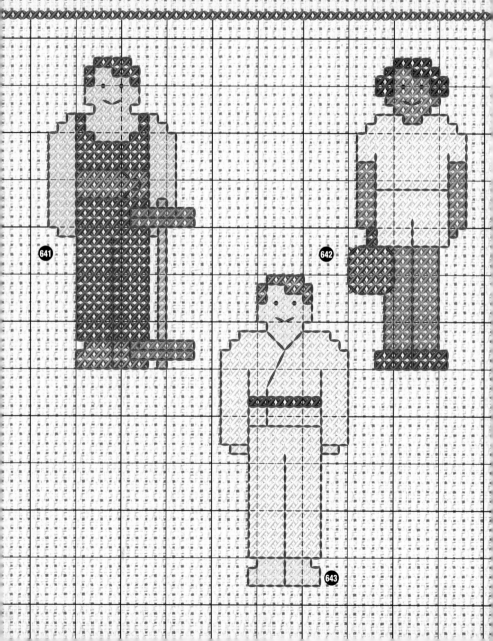

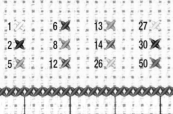

✕ 2   ✕ 10   ✕ 14   ✕ 33   ✕ 51
✕ 6   ✕ 11   ✕ 21   ✕ 37   ✕ 56
✕ 1   ✕ 8   ✕ 13   ✕ 31   ✕ 47   ✕ 57

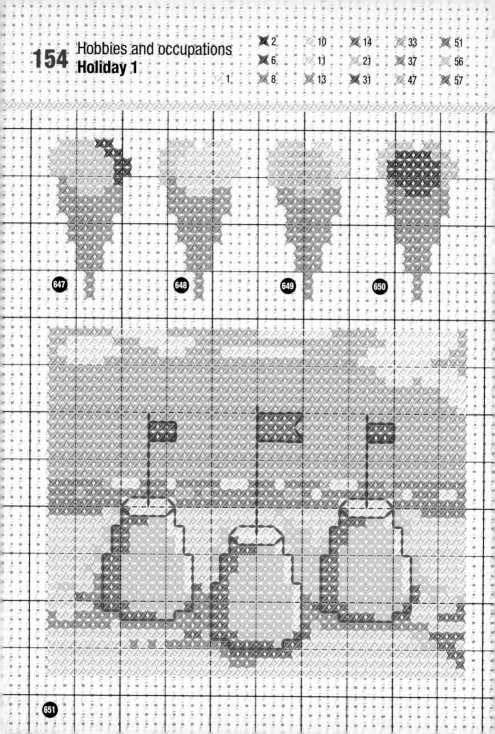

**647**   **648**   **649**   **650**

**651**

2 ✕   12 ✕   27 ✕   50 ✕   57 ✕
7 ✕   25 ✕   35 ✕   51 ✕
11 ✕   26 ✕   40 ✕   56 ✕

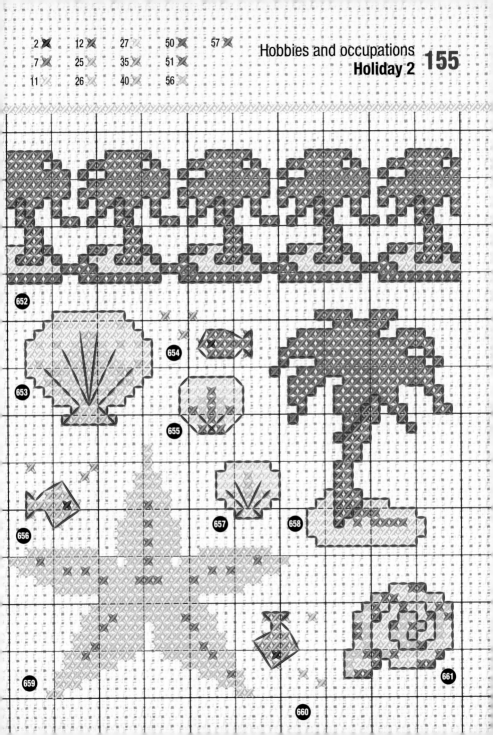

652
653
654
655
656
657
658
659
660
661

# Hobbies and occupations
## Boats 1

| | | | | |
|---|---|---|---|---|
| 2 | 7 | 10 | 16 | 56 |
| 4 | 8 | 11 | 31 | 57 |
| 5 | 9 | 14 | 33 | |

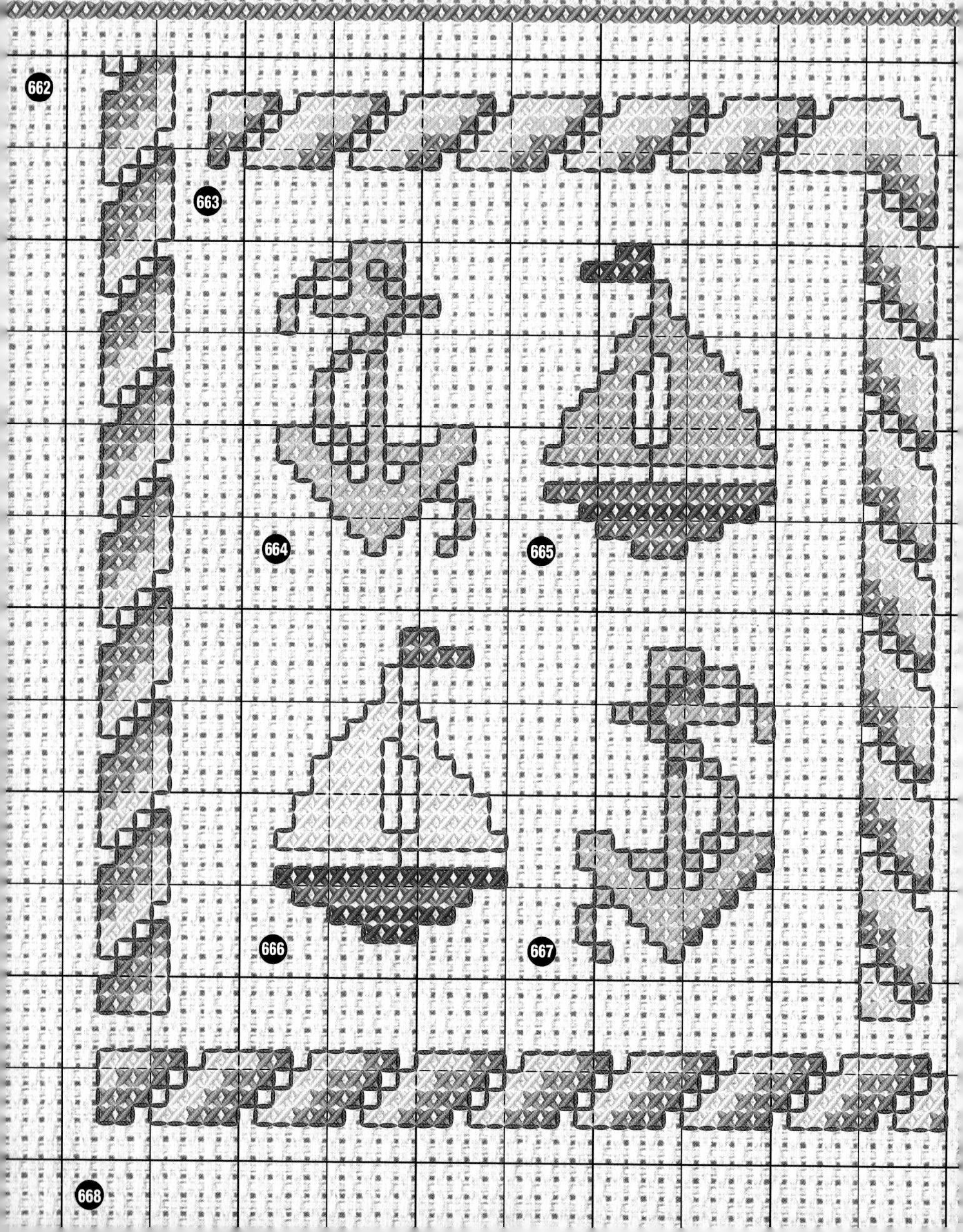

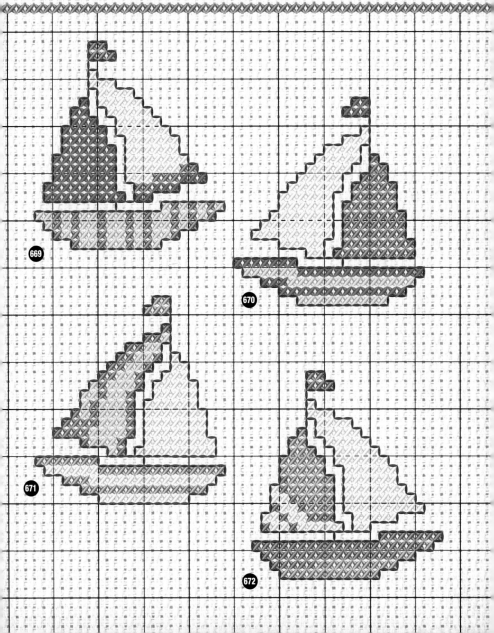

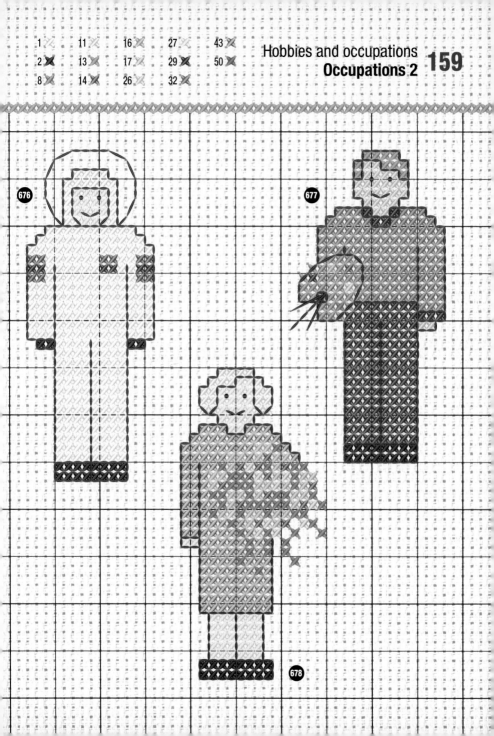

676

677

678

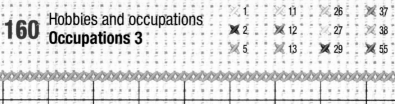

| | | | |
|---|---|---|---|
| ⊠ 1 | ⊠ 11 | ⊠ 26 | ⊠ 37 |
| ⊠ 2 | ⊠ 12 | 27 | ⊠ 38 |
| ⊠ 5 | ⊠ 13 | ⊠ 29 | ⊠ 55 |

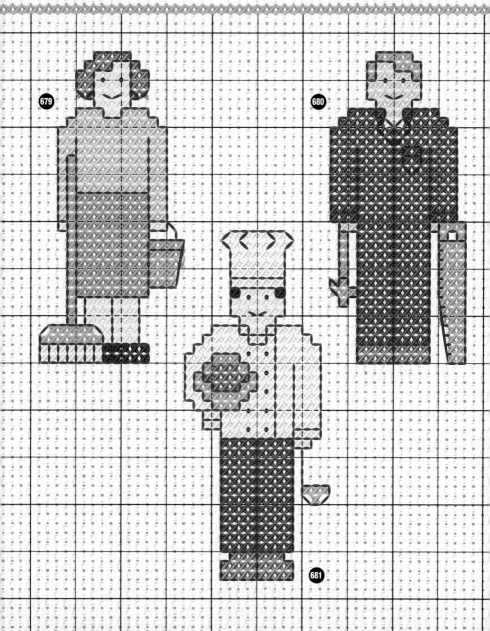

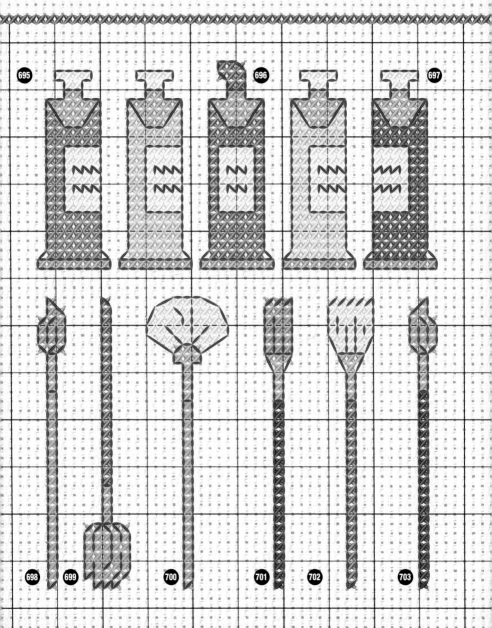

✗ 2  ✗ 13  ✗ 21  ✗ 31  ✗ 56
✗ 4  ✗ 15  ✗ 22  ✗ 50  ✗ 57
✗ 5  ✗ 17  ✗ 30  ✗ 51

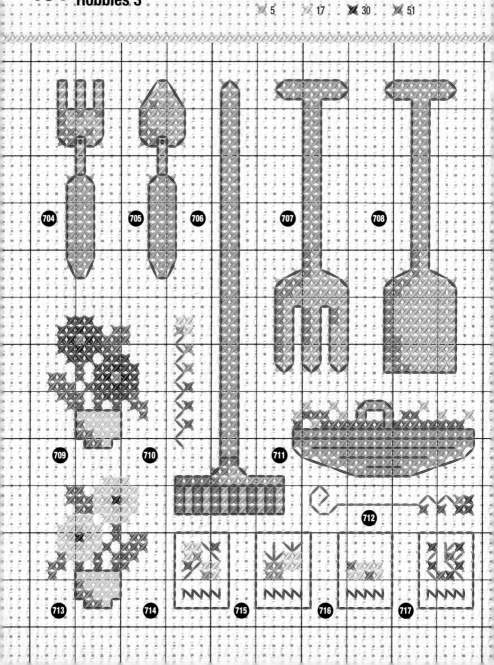

704  705  706  707  708

709  710  711

712

713  714  715  716  717

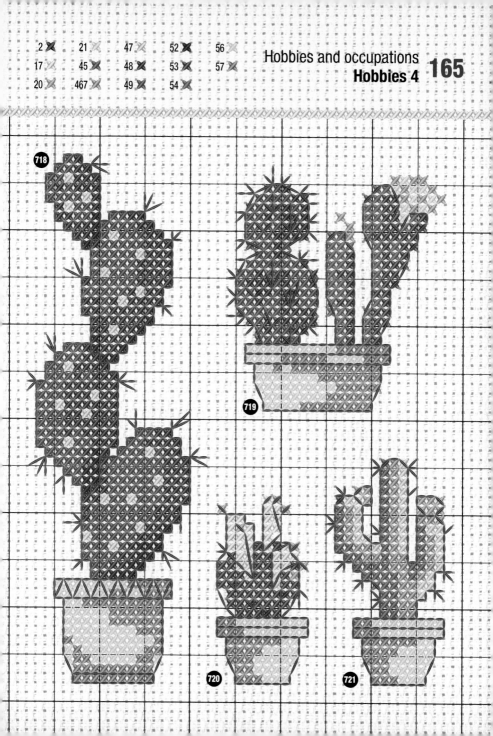

34
35

722
723
724
725
726
727

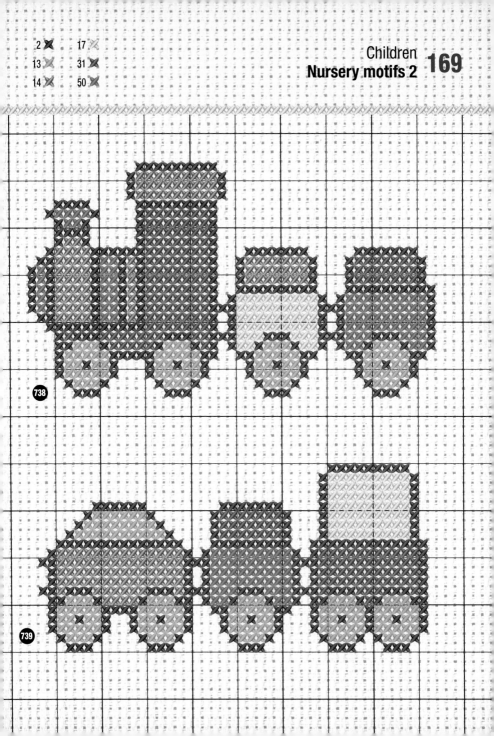

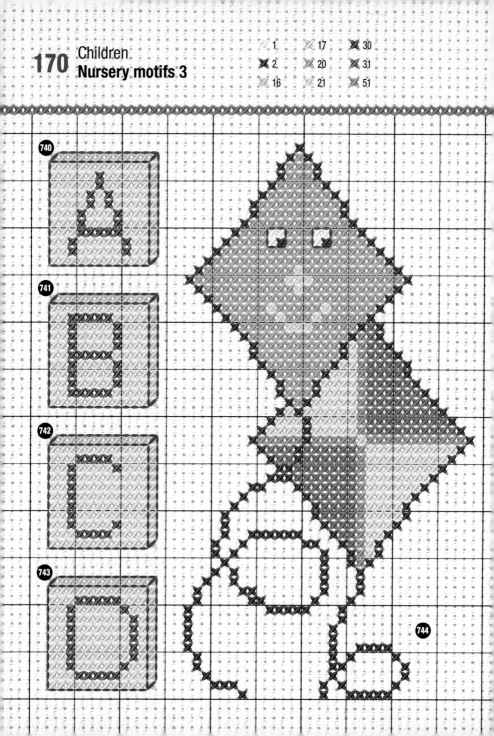

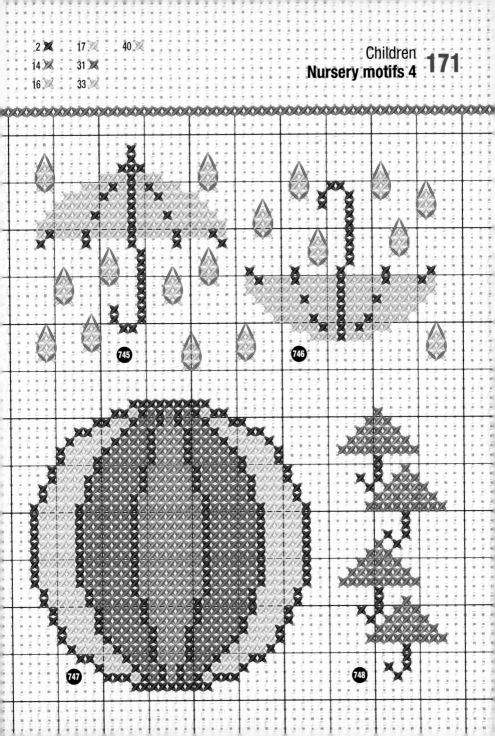

2 ✕  17 ✕  40 ✕
14 ✕  31 ✕
16 ✕  33 ✕

745

746

747

748

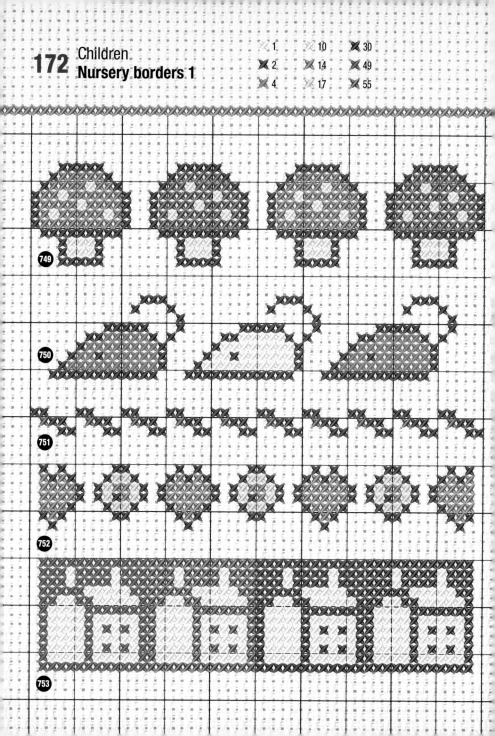

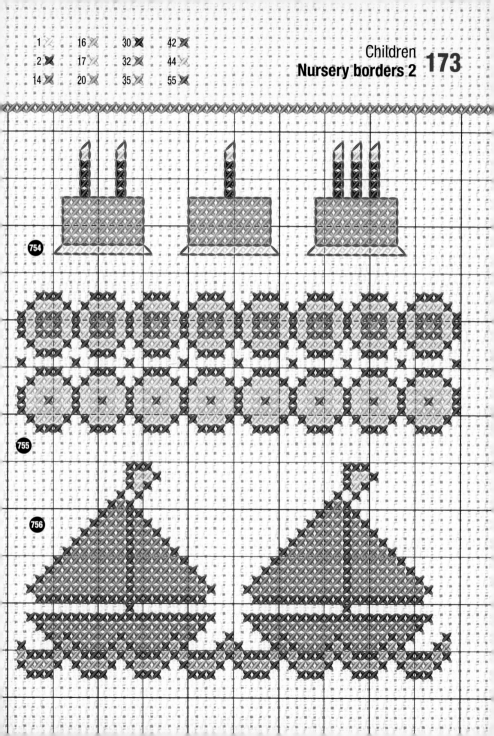

| 1 | 16 | 30 | 42 |
| 2 | 17 | 32 | 44 |
| 14 | 20 | 35 | 55 |

754

755

756

✖ 2   ✖ 12   ✖ 16   ✖ 31
✖ 6   ✖ 13   ✖ 26   ✖ 50
✖ 11   ✖ 14   ✖ 27

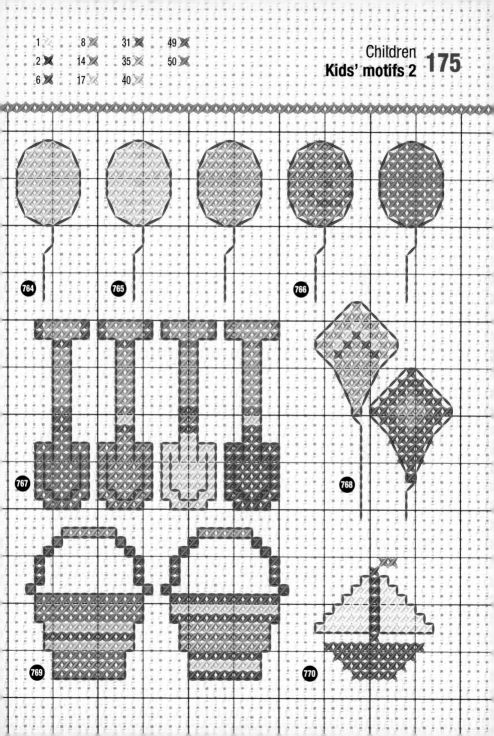

1 ⬙  8 ✕  31 ✕  49 ✕
2 ✕  14 ✕  35 ✕  50 ✕
6 ✕  17 ⬙  40 ⬙

764  765  766

767  768

769  770

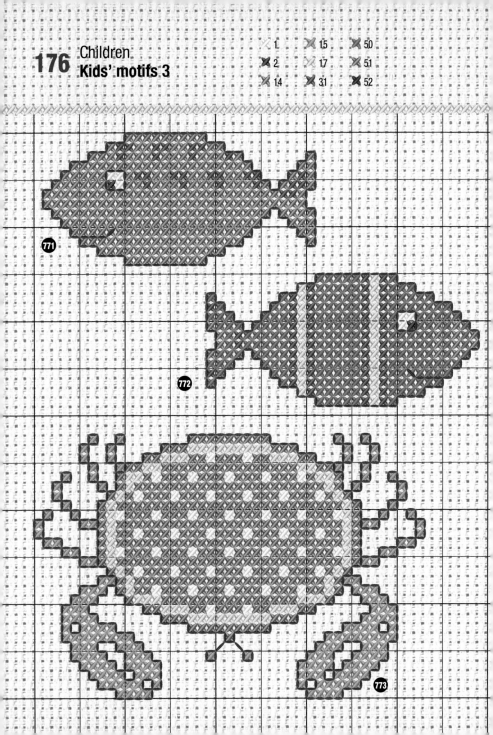

| | 1 | | 15 | | 50 |
|---|---|---|---|---|---|
| ✕ | 2 | | 17 | ✕ | 51 |
| | 14 | ✕ | 31 | ✕ | 52 |

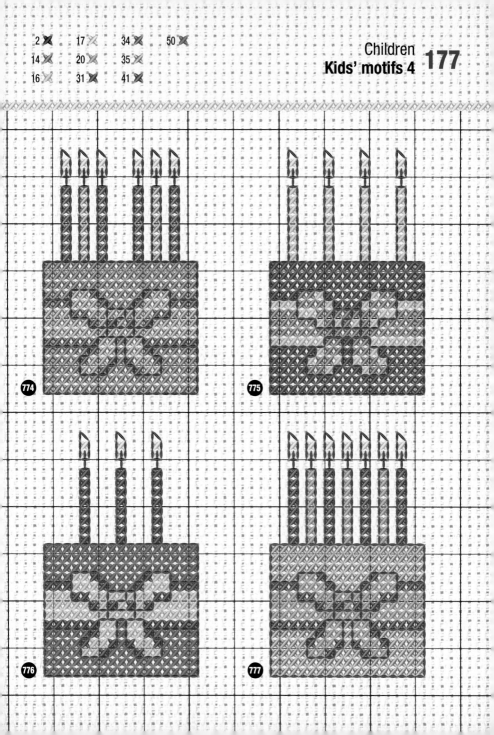

2 ✖  17 ✖  34 ✖  50 ✖
14 ✖  20 ✖  35 ✖
16 ✖  31 ✖  41 ✖

| | | | | | | | | | |
|---|---|---|---|---|---|---|---|---|---|
| ✕ 1 | | ✕ 14 | | ✕ 31 | | ✕ 41 | | ✕ 50 | |
| ✕ 2 | | ✕ 16 | | ✕ 35 | | ✕ 43 | | ✕ 55 | |
| ✕ 13 | | ✕ 17 | | ✕ 40 | | ✕ 49 | | | |

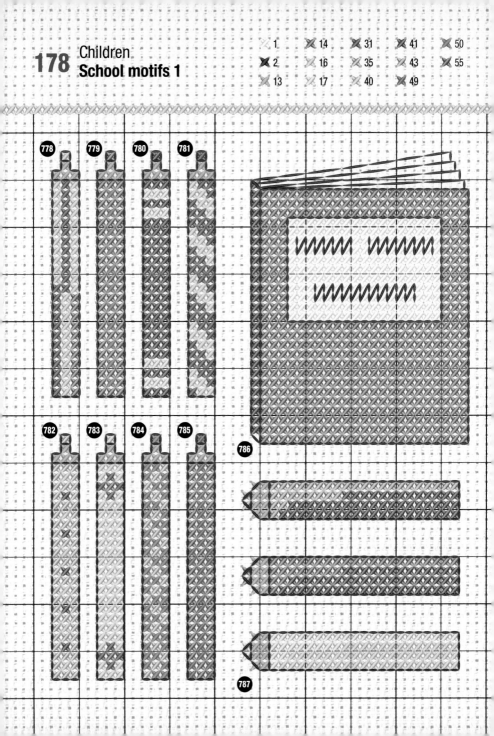

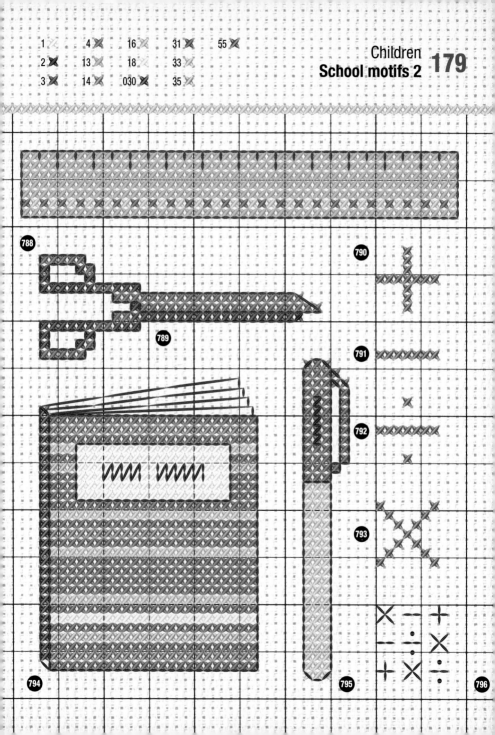

1    4 ✖    16 ✖    31 ✖    55 ✖
2 ✖    13 ✖    18 ✖    33 ✖
3 ✖    14 ✖    030 ✖    35 ✖

788

790

789

791

792

793

794     795     796

| ✖ 2 | ✖ 14 | ✖ 34 |
| ✖ 6 | ✖ 16 | ✖ 50 |
| ✖ 13 | ✖ 17 | ✖ 51 |

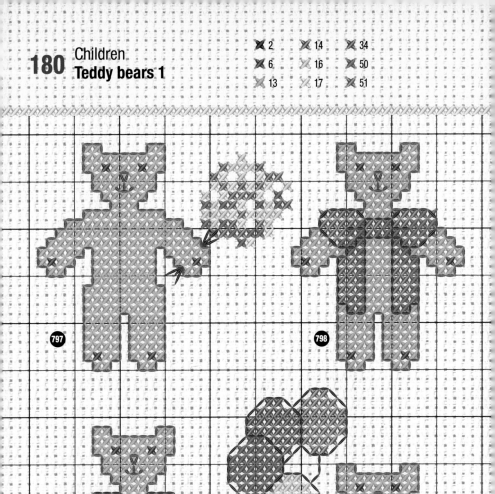

797
798
799
800

2 ✖  12 ✖  15 ✖  30 ✖  55 ✖
6 ✖  13 ✖  17 ✖  43 ✖
11 ✖  14 ✖  23 ✖  45 ✖

# 182 Children
## Teddy bears 3

| ✖ 2 | ✖ 12 | ✖ 18 | ✖ 51 |
| ✖ 6 | ✖ 13 | ✖ 26 | |
| ✖ 11 | ✖ 14 | ✖ 31 | |

804
805
806
807

1 ⌧ 11 ⌧ 14 ✖ 31 ✖
2 ✖ 12 ✖ 17 ⌧ 50 ✖
6 ✖ 13 ⌧ 30 ✖

809

808

810 811

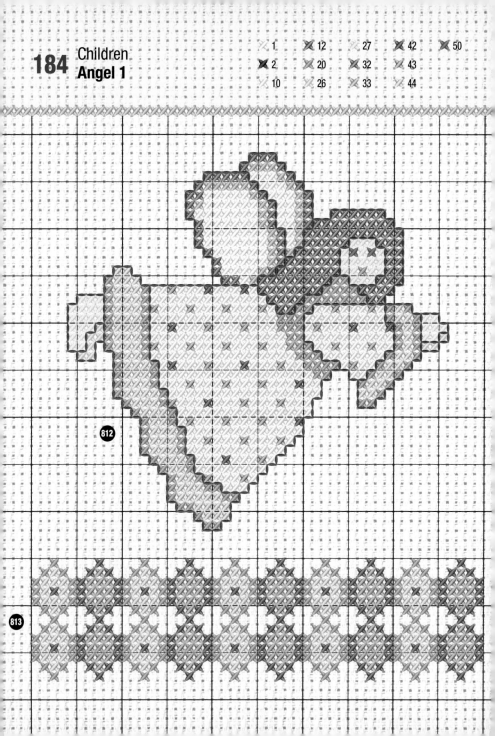

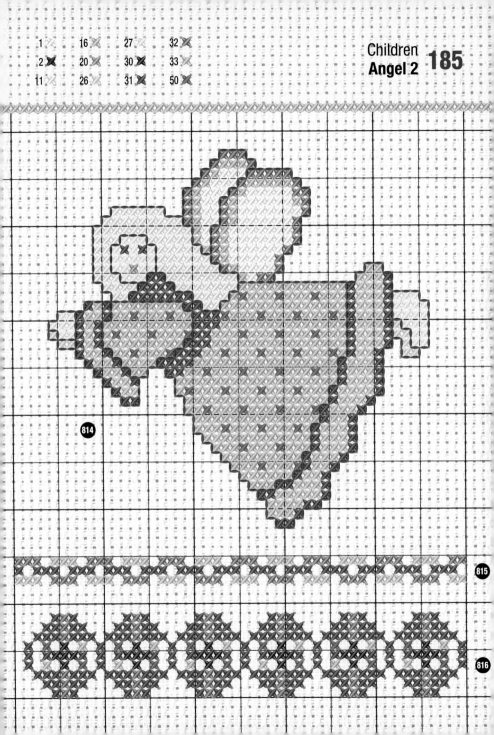

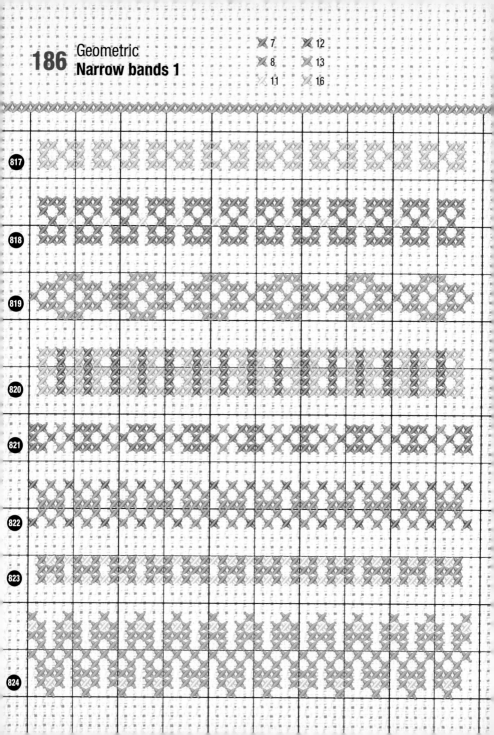

7  12
8  13
11  16

817
818
819
820
821
822
823
824

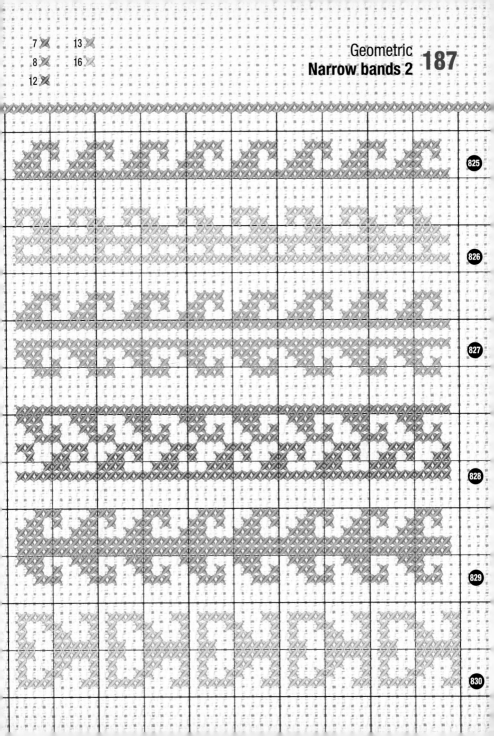

| | | | |
|---|---|---|---|
| ✖ 30 | ✖ 33 | ✖ 41 | |
| ✖ 31 | ✖ 36 | ✖ 43 | |
| ✖ 32 | ✖ 37 | | |

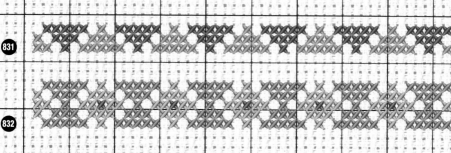

**831**

**832**

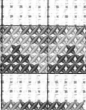

**833**

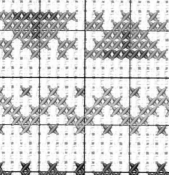

**834**

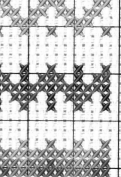

**835**

**836**

**837**

**838**

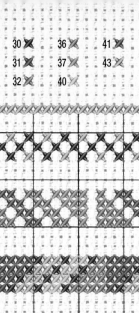

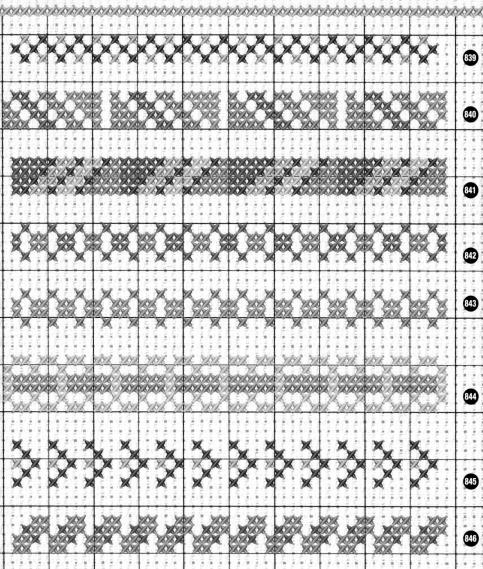

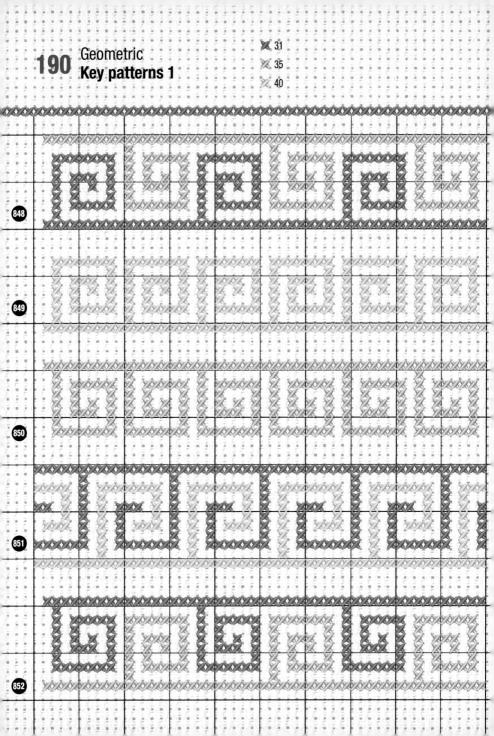

31
35
40

848
849
850
851
852

853

854

855

856

✕ 19   ✕ 22
✕ 20   ✕ 23
✕ 21   ✕ 25

858

857

859

860

861

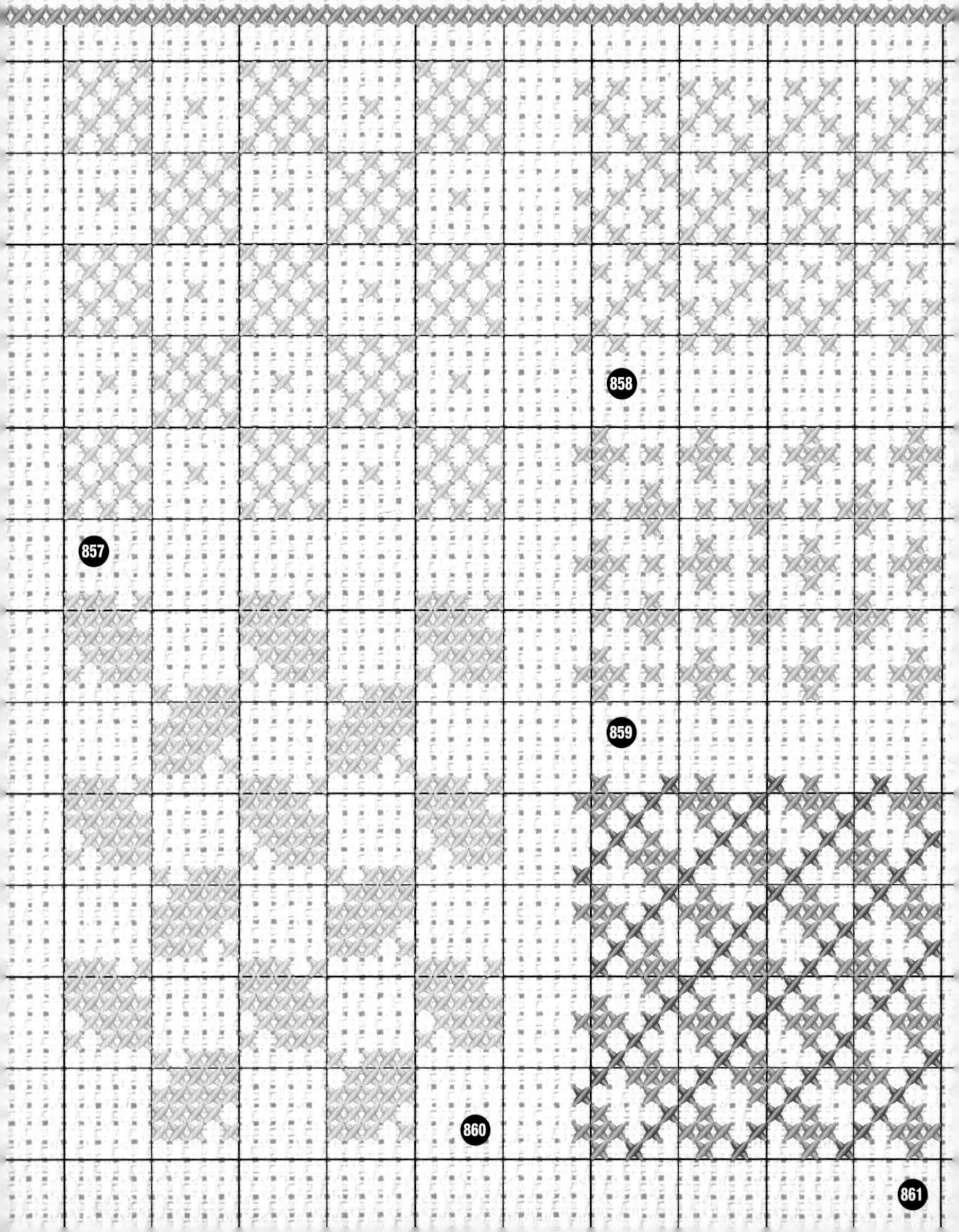

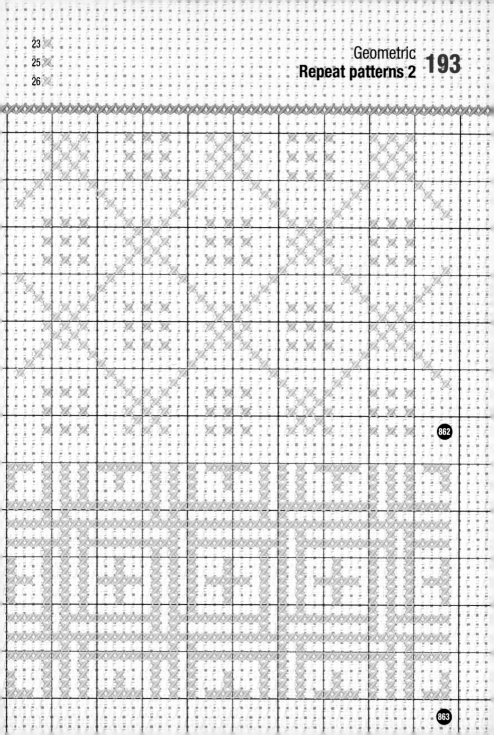

23
25
26

862

863

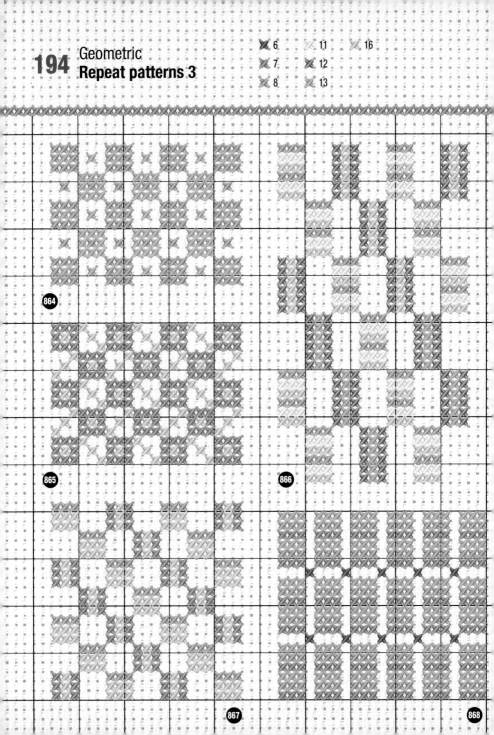

864

865

866

867

868

6 ✕    9 ✕    13 ✕

7 ✕    11 ✕    15 ✕

8 ✕    12 ✕    16 ✕

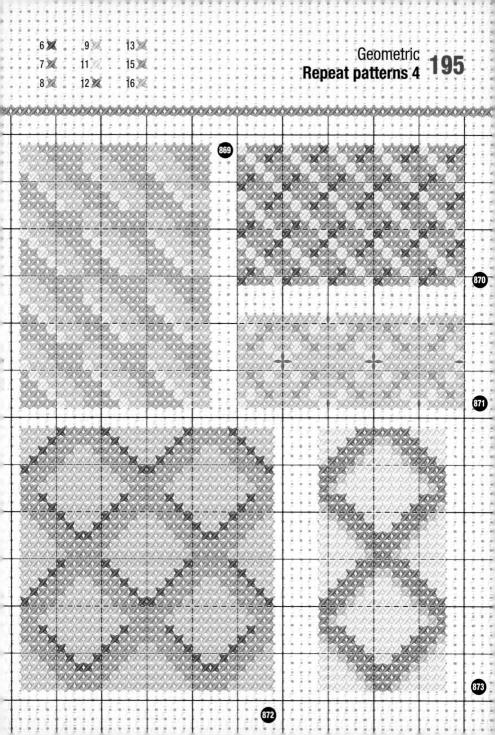

869

870

871

872

873

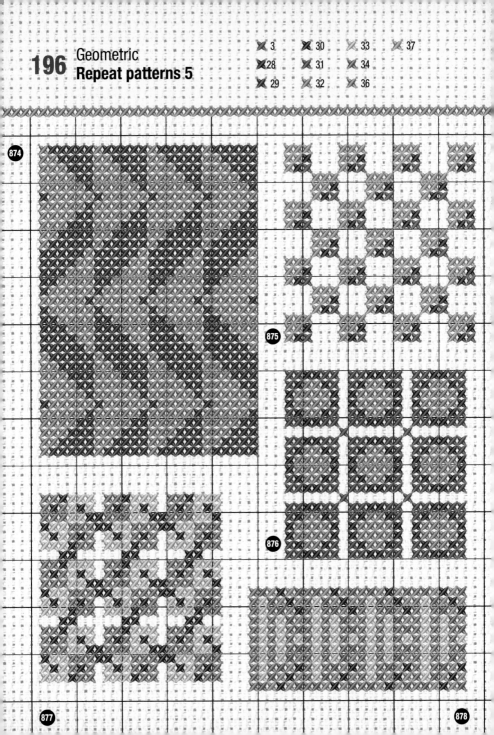

874 · 875 · 876 · 877 · 878

3 · 30 · 33 · 37
28 · 31 · 34
29 · 32 · 36

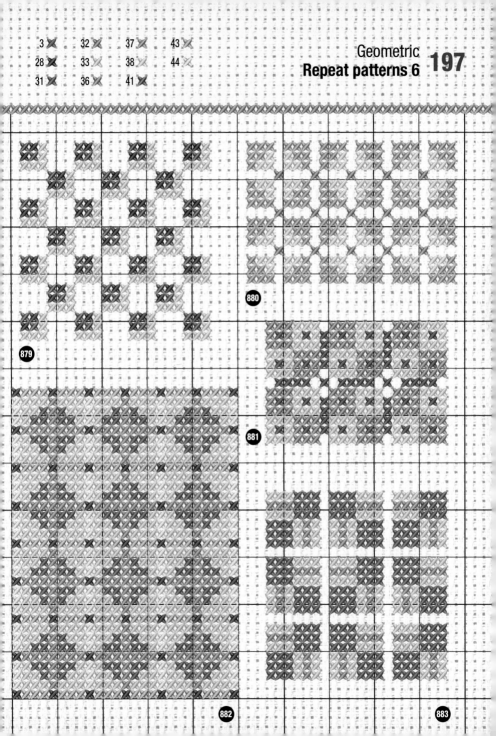

3 ✕  32 ✕  37 ✕  43 ✕
28 ✕  33 ✕  38 ✕  44 ✕
31 ✕  36 ✕  41 ✕

879

880

881

882

883

| | | | |
|---|---|---|---|
| ✖ 2 | ✖ 46 | ✖ 49 | ✖ 53 |
| ✖ 39 | ✖ 47 | ✖ 50 | ✖ 54 |
| ✖ 40 | ✖ 48 | ✖ 51 | |

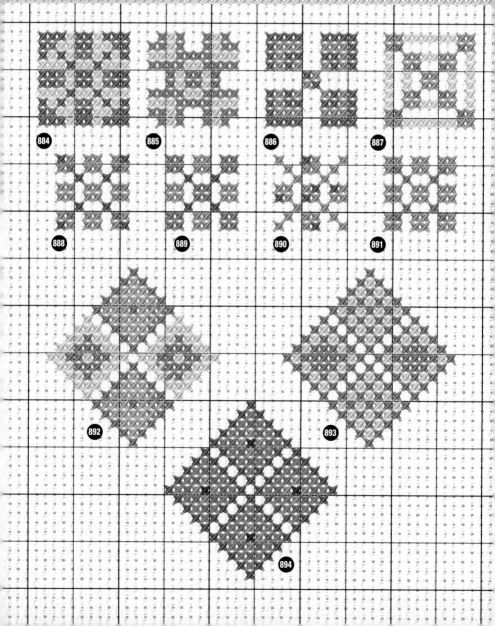

2 ✕  45 ✕  48 ✕  53 ✕
39 ✕  46 ✕  50 ✕  54 ✕
40 ✕  47 ✕  51 ✕

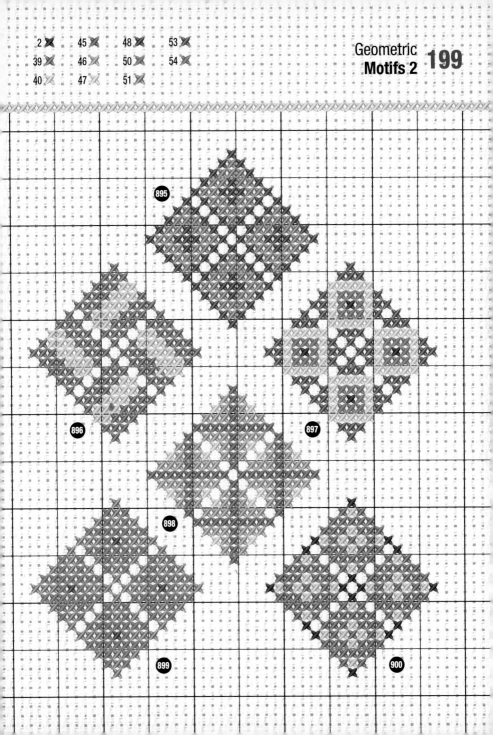

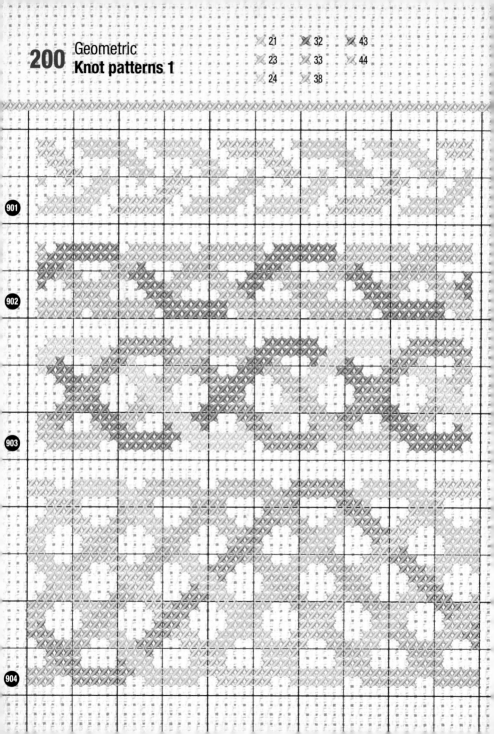

21    32    43
23    33    44
24    38

3 ✖   26 ✖   38 ✖
21 ✖   32 ✖   43 ✖
23 ✖   33 ✖   44 ✖

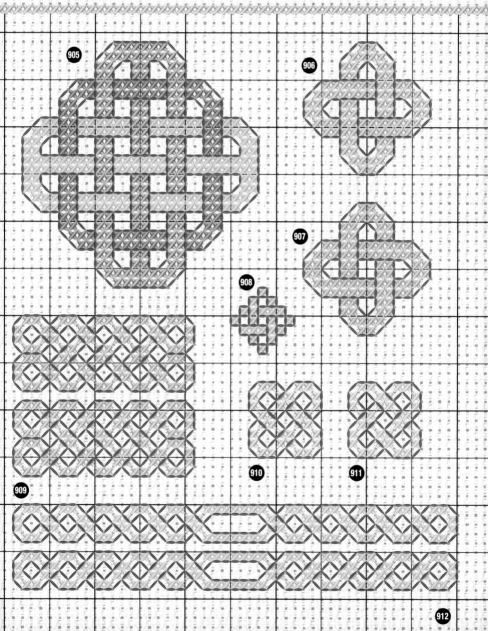

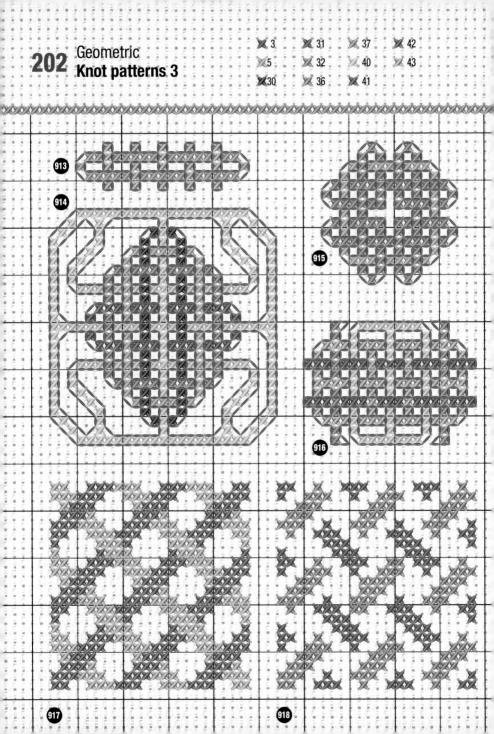

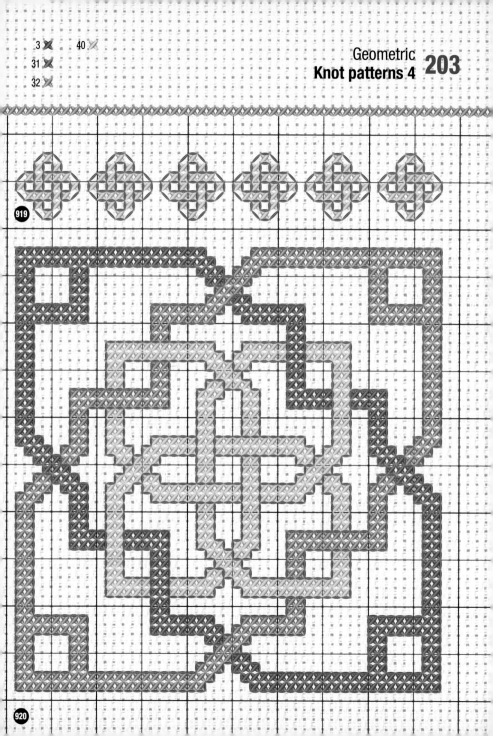

✖ 3  ✖ 21  ✖ 25
✖ 19  ✖ 22  ✖ 42
✖ 20  ✖ 24

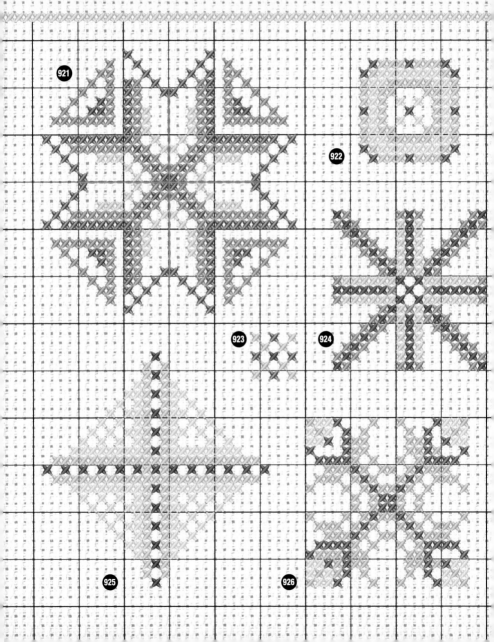

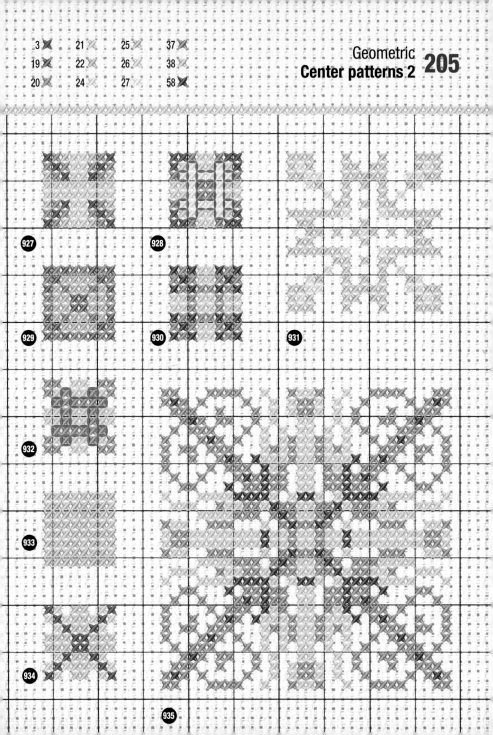

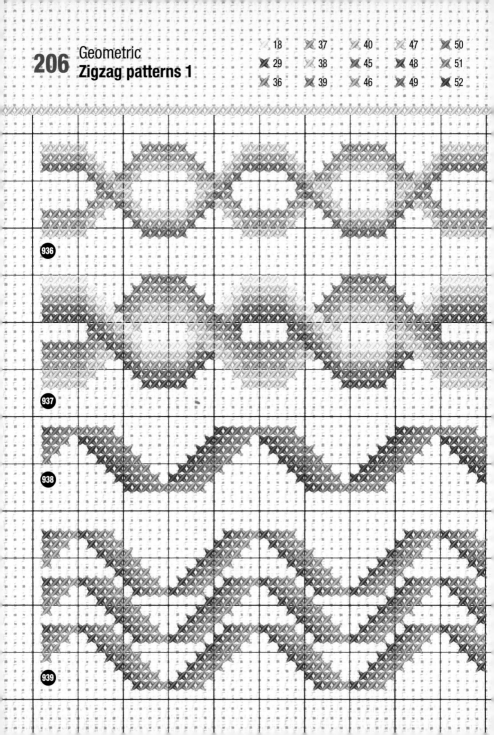

18    37    40    47    50
29    38    45    48    51
36    39    46    49    52

936

937

938

939

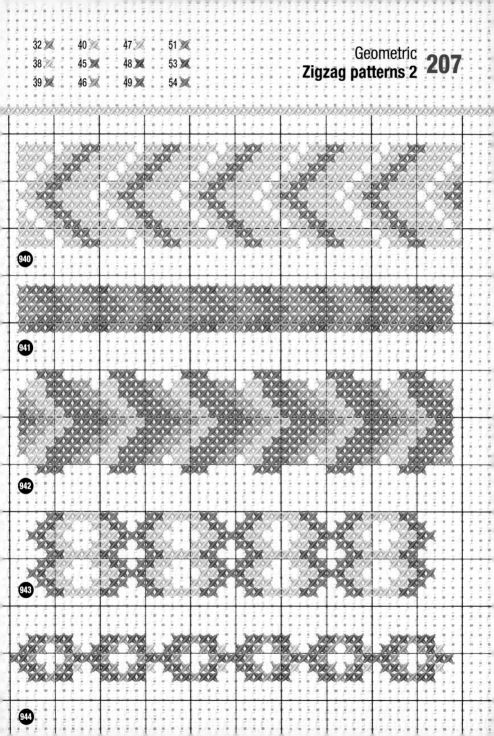

940

941

942

943

944

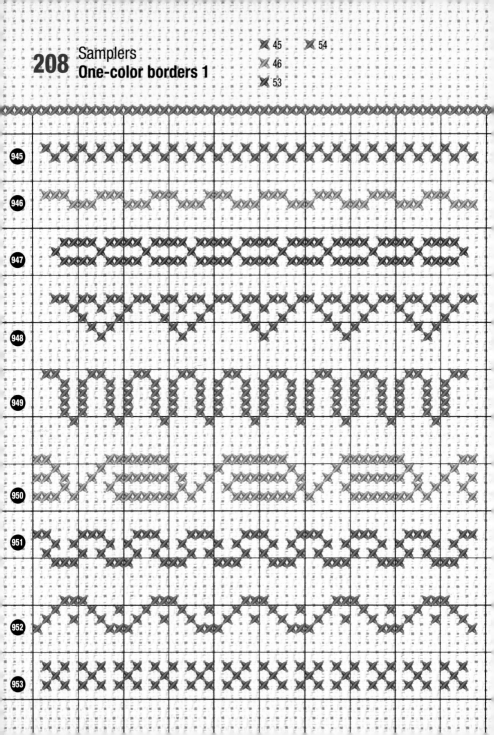

36 ✕  40 ✕
37 ✕
39 ✕

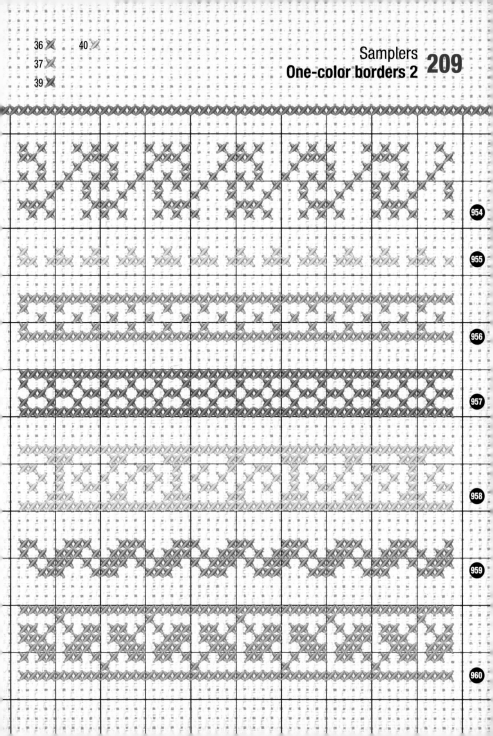

954
955
956
957
958
959
960

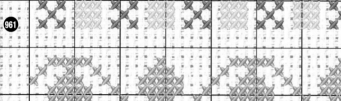

| | 20 | | 45 |
|---|---|---|---|
| | 23 | | 46 |
| | 43 | | 53 |

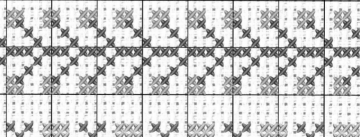

961

962

963

964

965

966

967

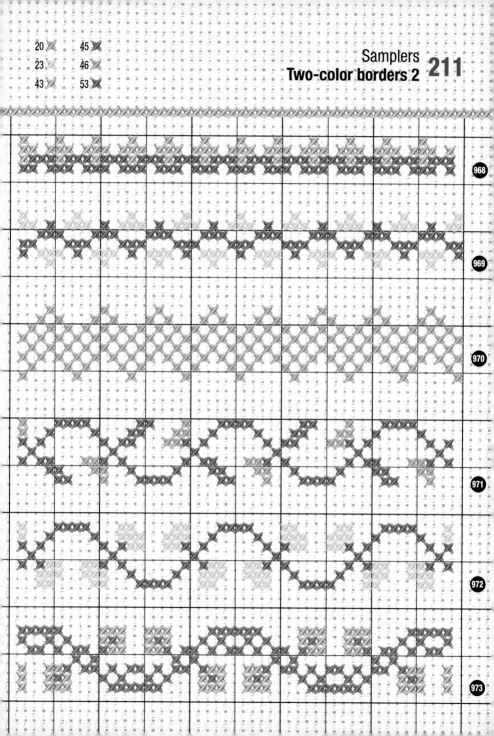

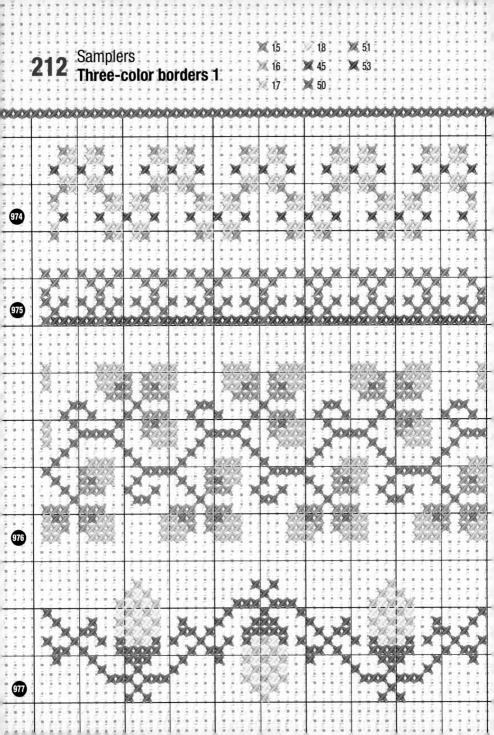

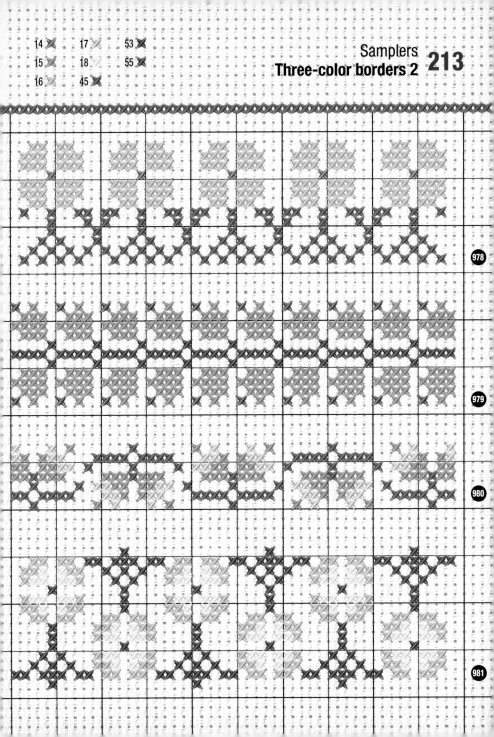

14 ✖  17 ✖  53 ✖
15 ✖  18 ✖  55 ✖
16 ✖  45 ✖

978

979

980

981

14 ✕   42 ✕   46 ✕
21 ✕   43 ✕   47 ✕
41 ✕   45 ✕   52 ✕

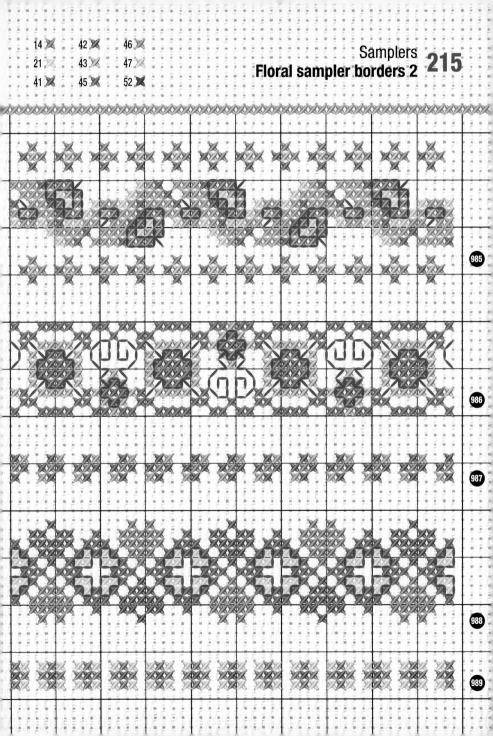

985

986

987

988

989

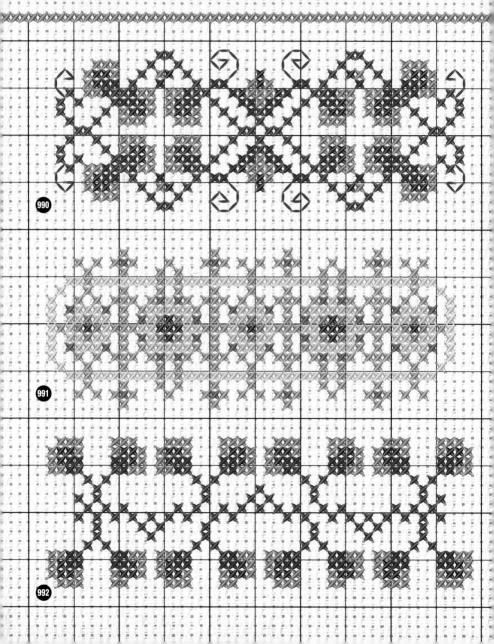

28 ✖   42 ✖   52 ✖
30 ✖   43 ✖   53 ✖
32 ✖   45 ✖

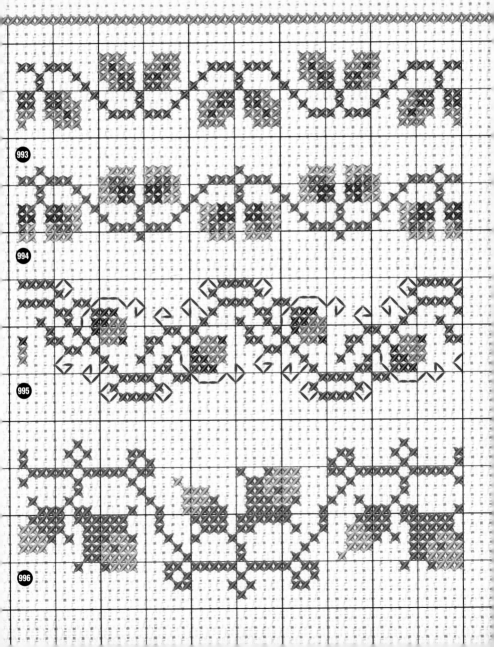

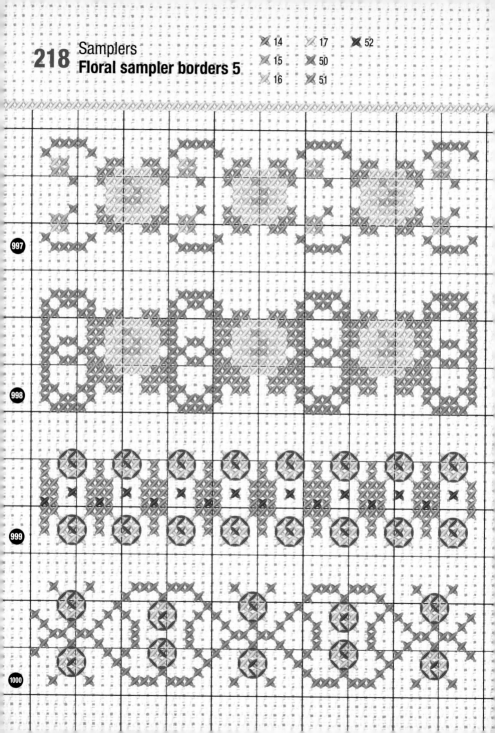

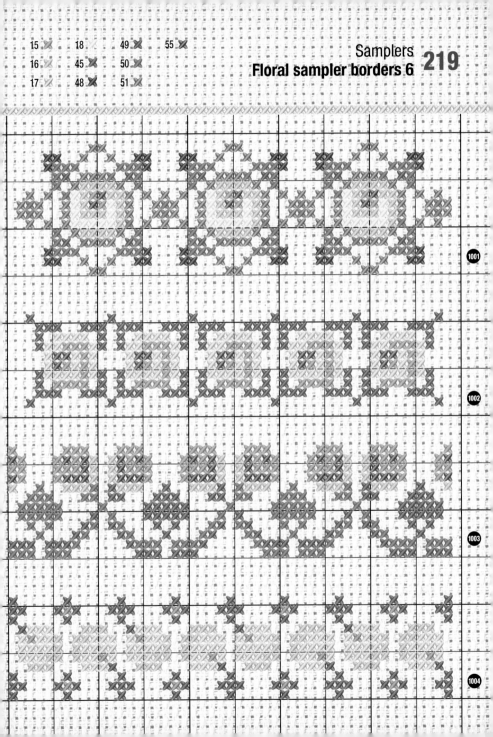

15 18 49 55
16 45 50
17 48 51

1001

1002

1003

1004

| 6 ✕ | 46 ✕ | 52 ✕ | 56 ✕ |
| 12 ✕ | 47 ✕ | 53 ✕ | 57 ✕ |
| 45 ✕ | 50 ✕ | 54 ✕ | |

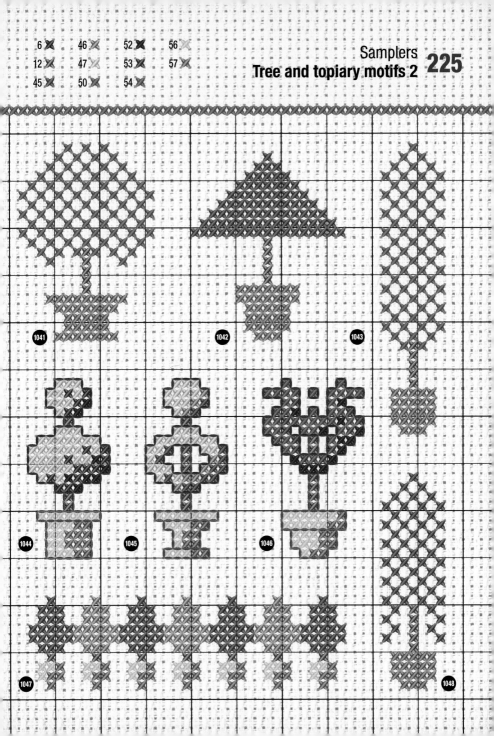

1041
1042
1043
1044
1045
1046
1047
1048

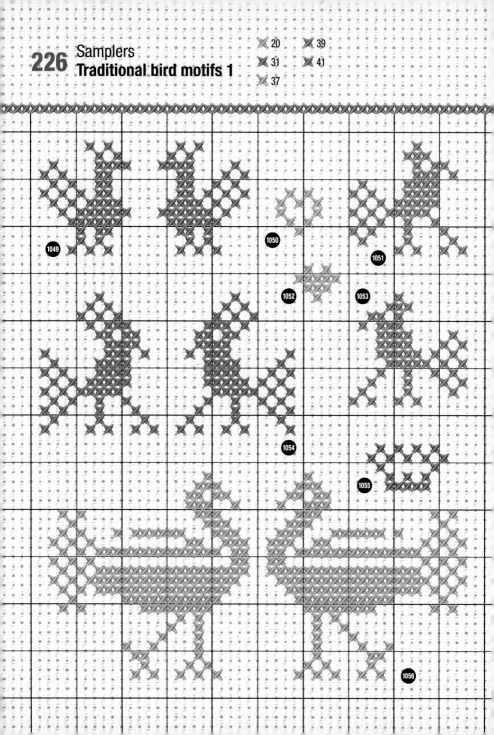

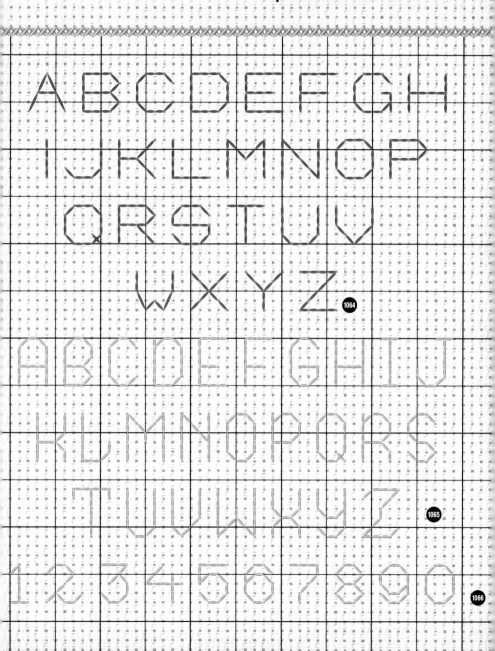

1064

1065

1066

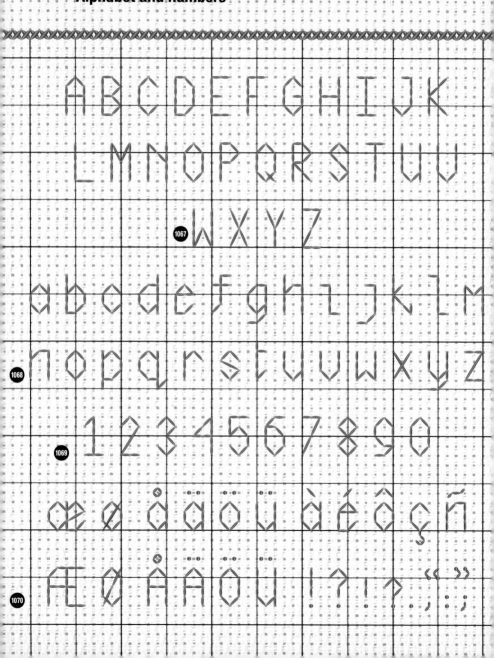

ABCDEFGHIJK
LMNOPQRSTUV
1067 WXYZ
abcdefghijkl m
1068 nopqrstuvwxyz
1069 1234567890
œøåāôu àéâçñ
1070 ÆØÅÂÔÜ !?!? «»,:;

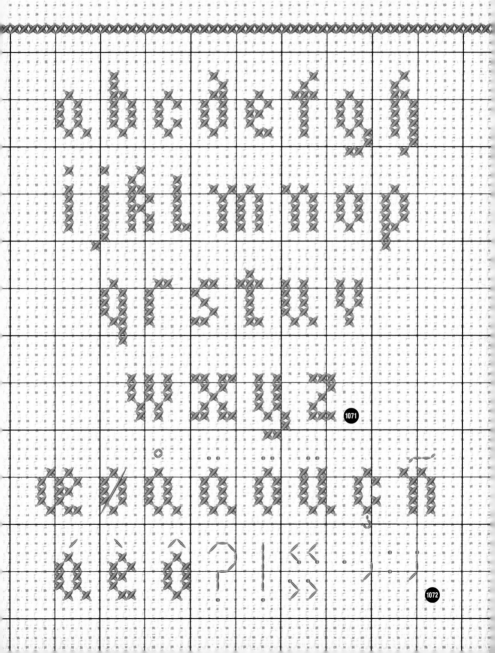

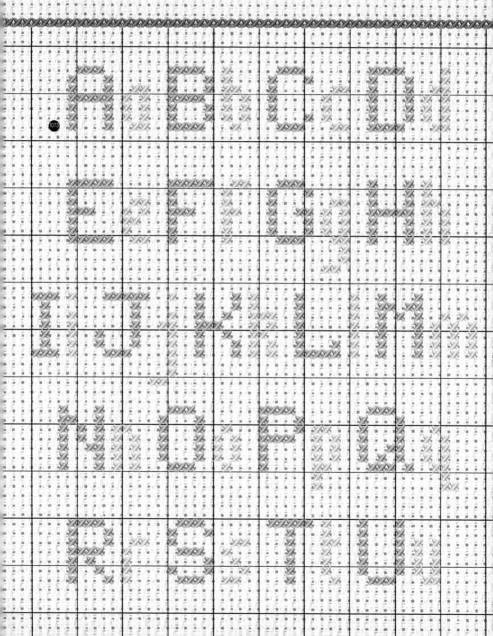

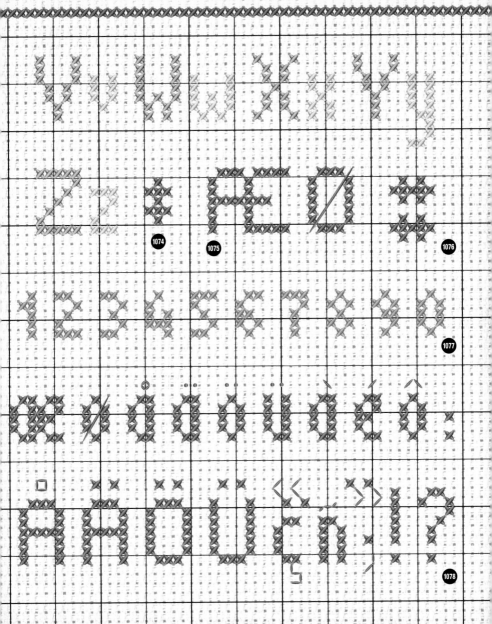

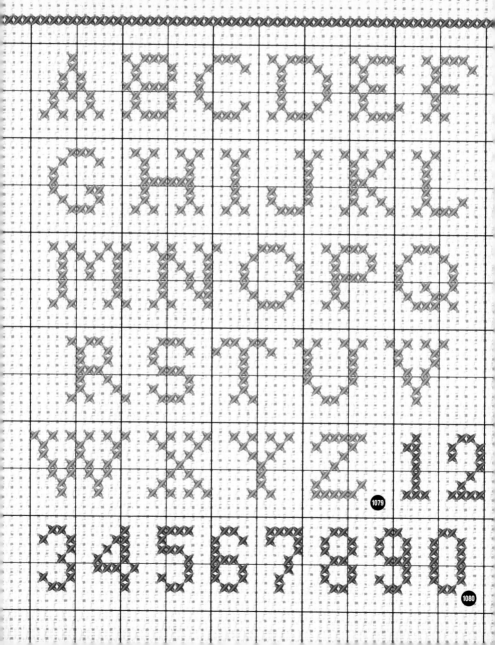

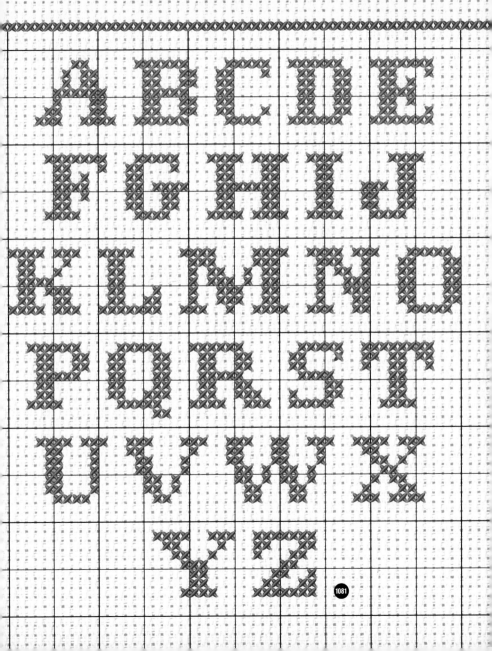

1081

✕ 12
✕ 13

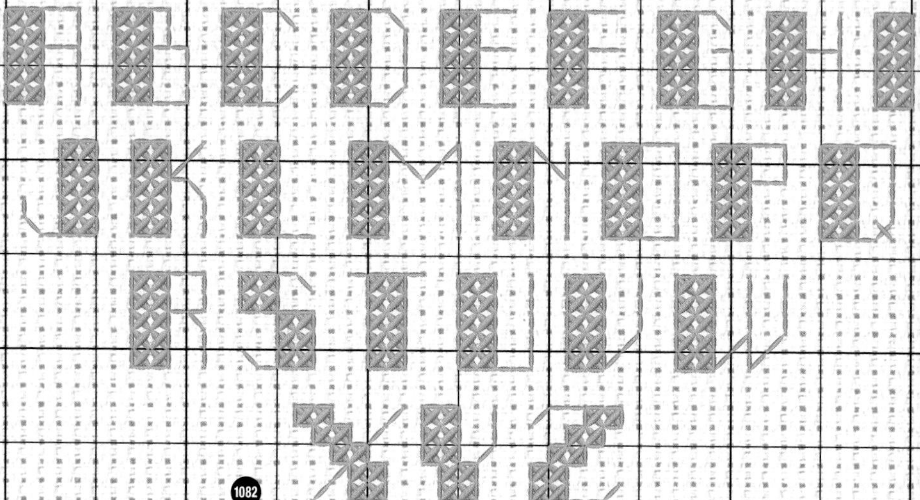

ABCDEFGHI
JKLMNOPQ
RSTUUW
XYZ

1082

ABCDEFG
HIJKLM
NOPQRST
UVWXYZ

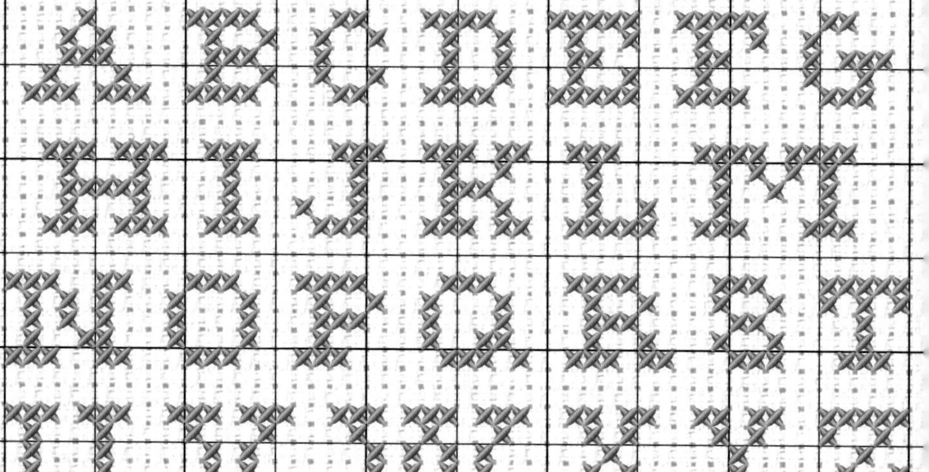

1083

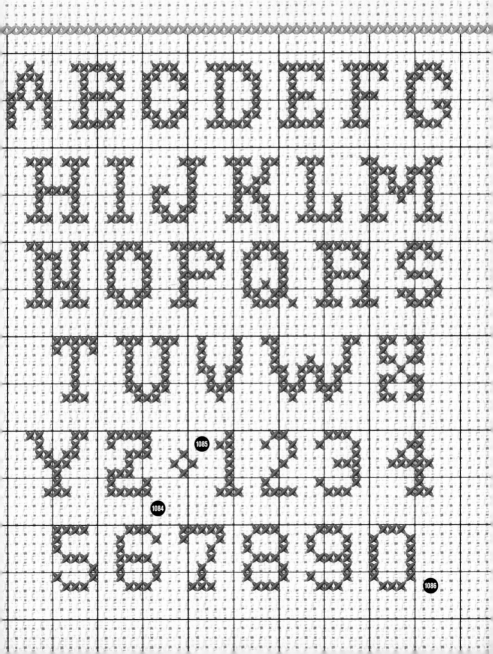

# 238 Stenciled alphabet

1087

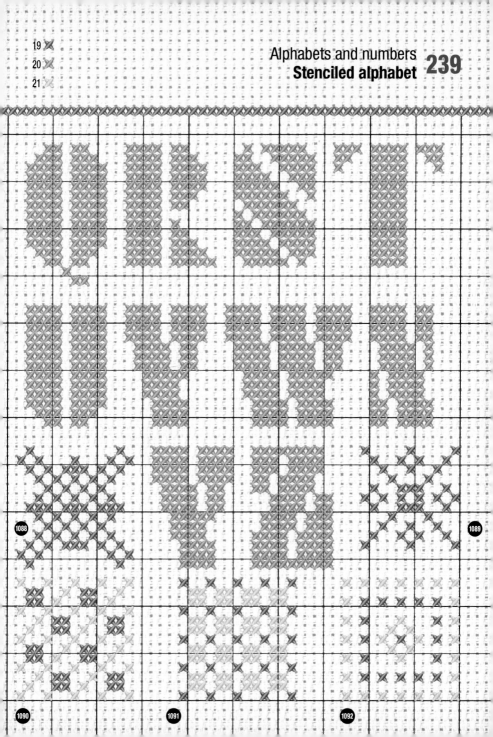

1093

31
32
38
40

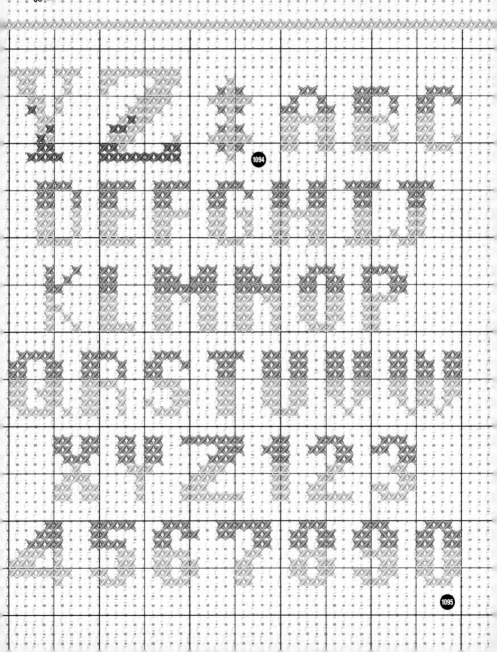

1094

1095

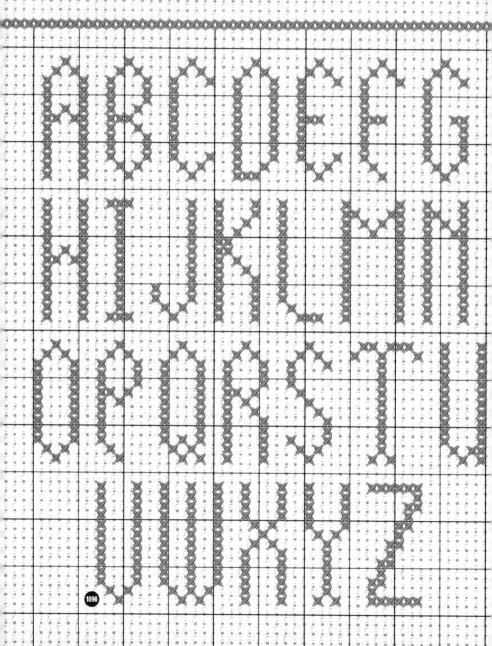

20  47
36 50
41

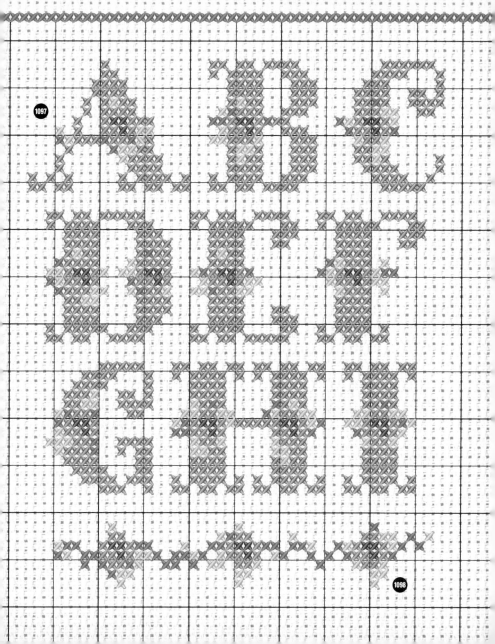

✕ 20    ✕ 47
✕ 36    ✕ 50
✕ 41

1099

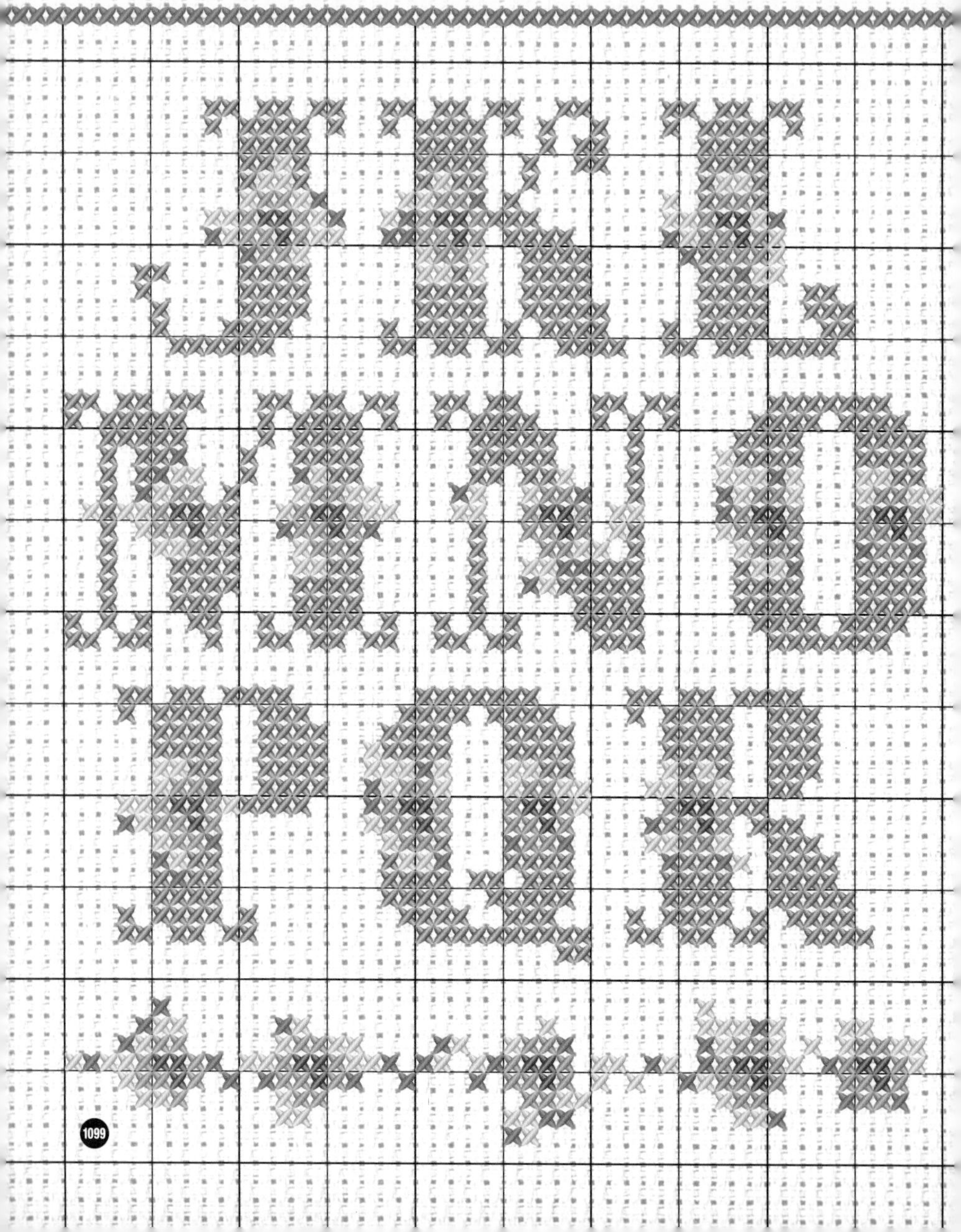

20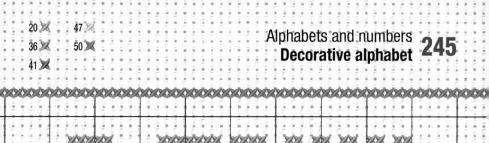
36
41
47
50

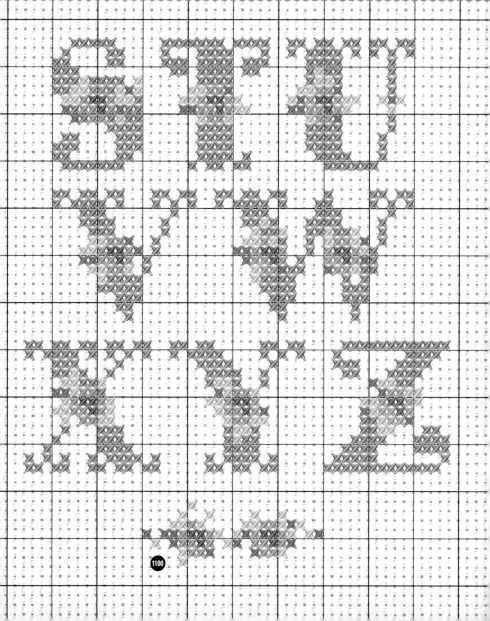

**246** Alphabets and numbers
## Decorative alphabet

3 · 16 · 17 · 28 · 29 · 32 · 46

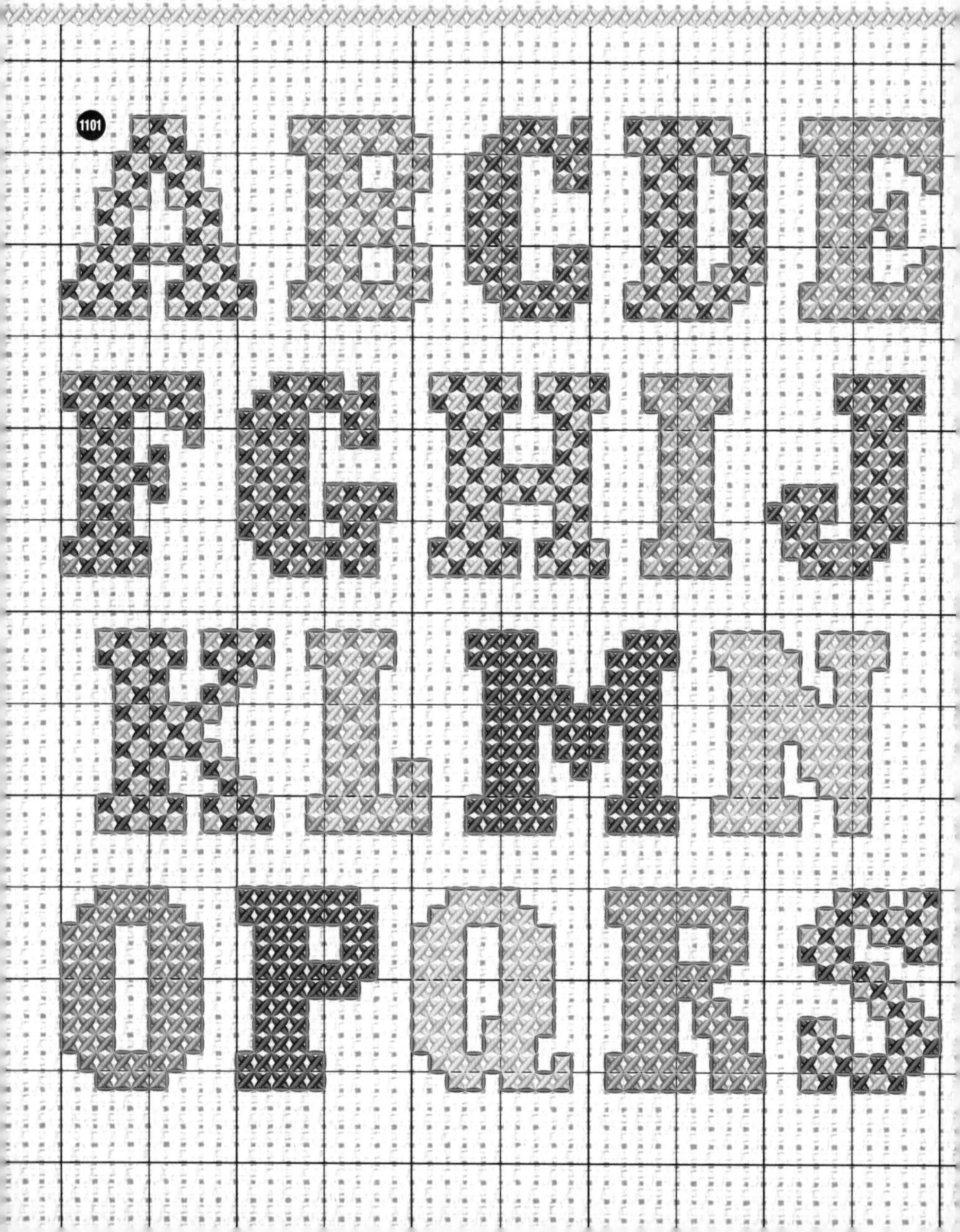

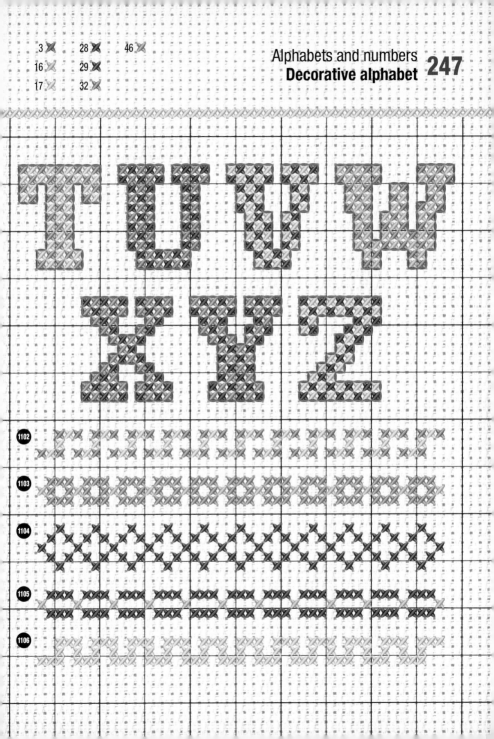

3 ✖  28 ✖  46 ✖
16 ✖  29 ✖
17 ✖  32 ✖

1102

1103

1104

1105

1106

✕ 12
✕ 13
✕ 15

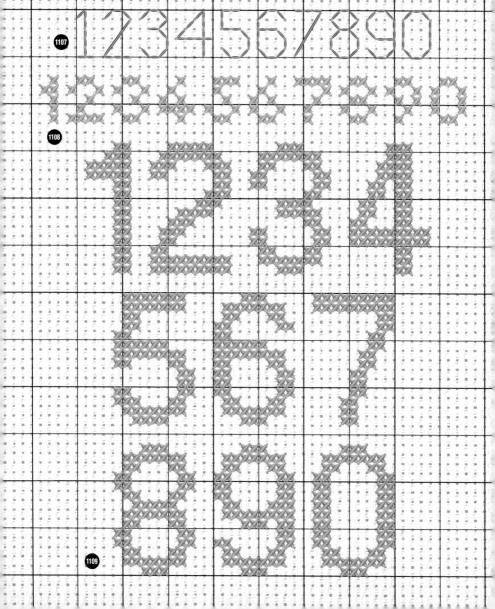

1107

1108

1109

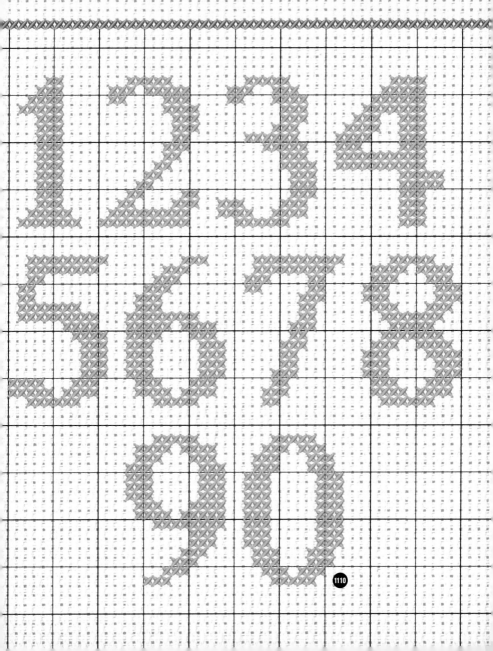

# 250
# List of sizes

Motif measurements are given as height x width, in numbers of stitches. Borders have either a height or width measurement, depending on the horizontal or vertical position of the border on the page. Alphabets and numbers have height measurements.

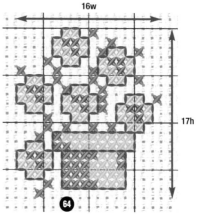

16w

17h

64

**FLOWERS**
1 42h x 8w
2 17h x 16w
3 16h x 17w
4 16h x 17w
5 17h x 16w
6 18h x 41w
7 18h x 12w
8 4h x 13w
9 4h x 18w
10 18h x 12w
11 14h x 8w
12 23h x 25w
13 13h x 6w
14 18h x 12w
15 4h x 18w
16 4h x 13w
17 18h x 12w
18 23h x 23w
19 18h x 17w
20 6w
21 12h
22 51h x 50w
23 28h
24 12h
25 11h
26 17h
27 12h x 11w
28 12h x 11w
29 12h x 11w
30 20h
31 20h
32 27h x 15w
33 33h x 33w
34 24h x 9w
35 15h
36 37h x 37w
37 37h x 8w

38 32h x 33w
39 19h x 8w
40 9h x 13w
41 5h
42 15h
43 23h x 22w
44 24h x 24w
45 18h x 17w
46 18h x 17w
47 18h x 17w
48 11w
49 49h x 29w
50 49h x 29w
51 6w
52 39h x 39w
53 13h x 13w
54 13h x 13w
55 13h x 13w
56 24h x 24w
57 24h x 24w
58 23h x 23w
59 12w
60 14h x 14w
61 14h x 14w
62 39h x 34w
63 50h x 22w
64 50h x 22w
65 18h x 16w
66 17h
67 17h
68 19h
69 4h
70 7h
71 8h
72 9h
73 7h
74 7h
75 13h

76 18h
77 18h
78 10h
79 20h
80 20h

**HOME AND GARDEN**
81 38h x 21w
82 38h x 21w
83 7h x 7w
84 17h x 26w
85 21h x 26w
86 21h x 26w
87 5h x 15w
88 4h x 6w
89 43h x 22w
90 23h x 25w
91 43h x 22w
92 12h x 48w
93 23h x 45w
94 33h x 43w
95 17h x 20w
96 15h x 24w
97 18h x 30w
98 18h x 11w
99 14h x 42w
100 44h x 19w
101 46h x 21w
102 16h x 6w
103 16h x 6w
104 16h x 6w
105 16h x 6w
106 16h x 6w
107 4h
108 12h
109 16h x 6w
110 16h x 6w

111 16h x 6w
112 16h x 6w
113 16h x 6w
114 16h x 6w
115 16h x 6w
116 16h x 6w
117 16h x 6w
118 16h x 6w
119 3h x 8w
120 3h x 8w
121 6h x 7w
122 6h x 7w
123 7h x 2w
124 2h x 7w
125 2h x 7w
126 7h x 2w
127 6h x 11w
128 6h x 11w
129 18h x 8w
130 18h x 8w
131 18h x 8w
132 18h x 8w
133 12h x 10w
134 12h x 10w
135 12h x 10w
136 12h x 10w
137 12h x 10w
138 12h x 10w
139 12h x 10w
140 12h x 10w
141 12h x 10w
142 12h x 10w
143 12h x 10w
144 12h x 10w
145 12h x 10w
146 12h x 10w
147 12h x 10w
148 12h x 10w

149 12h x 17w
150 12h x 17w
151 13h x 6w
152 20h x 11w
153 16h x 12w
154 26h x 22w
155 26h x 22w
156 15h x 15w
157 21h x 17w
158 17h x 11w
159 17h x 11w
160 36h x 20w
161 14h x 9w
162 14h x 9w
163 10w
164 5h x 5w
165 9h x 9w
166 8h x 8w
167 31h x 29w
168 4w
169 28h x 13w
170 28h x 13w
171 21h x 29w
172 17h x 10w
173 28h x 37w
174 16h x 18w
175 9w
176 41h x 41w
177 13h x 24w
178 13h x 24w
179 36h x 38w
180 33h x 15w
181 20h x 8w
182 19h x 15w
183 17h x 7w
184 17h x 7w
185 27h x 11w
186 17h x 6w

187 17h x 6w
188 27h x 9w
189 17h x 6w
190 17h x 6w
191 13h x 14w
192 5h
193 22h x 30w
194 4h x 4w
195 33h x 10w
196 46h x 44w
197 9h x 13w
198 9h x 13w
199 9h x 13w
200 46h x 44w
201 9h x 13w
202 9h x 13w
203 9h x 13w

**NATURAL WORLD**
204 36h x 35w
205 32h x 15w
206 20h x 20w
207 22h x 22w
208 26h x 25w
209 17h x 17w
210 13h x 13w
211 15h x 15w
212 32h x 32w
213 23h x 23w
214 16h x 12w
215 18h x 18w
216 25h x 23w
217 15h x 12w
218 7w
219 19h x 24w
220 10h x 15w
221 8h x 16w

**525** 25h
**526** 21h x 32w
**527** 13h
**528** 13h
**529** 13h
**530** 12h
**531** 12h
**532** 13h
**533** 13h
**534** 11h

**HISTORY**
**535** 56h x 31w
**536** 16h x 13w
**537** 30h x 8w
**538** 31h x 25w
**539** 13h
**540** 11h
**541** 9h x 6w
**542** 26h x 17w
**543** 12h x 10w
**544** 26h x 17w
**545** 31h x 23w
**546** 31h x 23w
**547** 4h x 9w
**548** 21h x 14w
**549** 4h x 9w
**550** 22h
**551** 8w
**552** 22h x 34w
**553** 10h
**554** 22h x 34w
**555** 21h x 21w
**556** 26h x 24w
**557** 26h x 26w
**558** 23h x 26w
**559** 26h x 24w
**560** 26h x 26w
**561** 9h x 49w
**562** 43h x 43w
**563** 44h x 44w
**564** 7h
**565** 17h x 17w
**566** 17h x 17w
**567** 21h x 50w
**568** 11h x 47w
**569** 56h x 44w
**570** 28h x 10w
**571** 28h x 10w
**572** 25h
**573** 26h x 21w

**574** 28h x 23w
**575** 8w
**576** 29h x 37w
**577** 8h
**578** 16h
**579** 15w
**580** 16h x 25w
**581** 38h x 27w
**582** 21h
**583** 21h
**584** 9h
**585** 4h
**586** 7h
**587** 20h x 20w
**588** 19h x 19w
**589** 8h
**590** 4h
**591** 9h
**592** 7h
**593** 5h
**594** 8h
**595** 12h
**596** 16h x 16w
**597** 16h x 16w
**598** 16h x 16w
**599** 16h x 16w
**600** 16h x 16w
**601** 16h x 16w
**602** 8w
**603** 17h x 17w
**604** 17h x 17w
**605** 17h x 17w
**606** 17h x 17w
**607** 5w
**608** 3h
**609** 12h
**610** 30h x 33w
**611** 19h x 8w
**612** 19h x 8w
**613** 23h x 23w
**614** 8w
**615** 5w
**616** 5w
**617** 17h x 19w
**618** 17h x 19w
**619** 24h x 24w
**620** 5w
**621** 9h x 7w
**622** 30h x 33w
**623** 42h x 46w
**624** 10h x 15w

**625** 11h x 34w
**626** 3h
**627** 15h x 31w
**628** 7h x 11w
**629** 10h x 10w
**630** 12w
**631** 5h x 5w
**632** 5h x 5w
**633** 10h x 10w
**634** 29h x 29w

**HOBBIES AND**
**OCCUPATIONS**
**635** 34h x 16w
**636** 33h x 15w
**637** 33h x 14w
**638** 33h x 13w
**639** 33h x 12w
**640** 43h x 12w
**641** 33h x 16w
**642** 33h x 13w
**643** 33h x 14w
**644** 34h x 17w
**645** 33h x 14w
**646** 33h x 14w
**647** 17h x 17w
**648** 17h x 17w
**649** 17h x 17w
**650** 17h x 17w
**651** 37h x 46w
**652** 14h
**653** 12h x 14w
**654** 5h x 10w
**655** 6h x 7w
**656** 7h x 8w
**657** 6h x 7w
**658** 25h x 20w
**659** 27h x 31w
**660** 8h x 8w
**661** 10h x 12w
**662** 4w
**663** 4w
**664** 17h x 11w
**665** 17h x 13w
**666** 17h x 13w
**667** 17h x 11w
**668** 4h
**669** 22h x 21w
**670** 22h x 21w
**671** 22h x 21w
**672** 22h x 21w

**673** 33h x 14w
**674** 33h x 12w
**675** 33h x 14w
**676** 35h x 14w
**677** 33h x 17w
**678** 33h x 16w
**679** 33h x 16w
**680** 33h x 15w
**681** 37h x 16w
**682** 33h x 15w
**683** 33h x 20w
**684** 33h x 15w
**685** 11h x 20w
**686** 4h x 4w
**687** 7h
**688** 19h x 19w
**689** 4h x 4w
**690** 7h
**691** 8h x 18w
**692** 15h x 21w
**693** 5h x 31w
**694** 12h x 10w
**695** 21h x 8w
**696** 22h x 8w
**697** 21h x 8w
**698** 31h x 3w
**699** 31h x 5w
**700** 31h x 9w
**701** 31h x 3w
**702** 31h x 5w
**703** 31h x 3w
**704** 21h x 5w
**705** 21h x 5w
**706** 46h x 12w
**707** 31h x 8w
**708** 31h x 8w
**709** 14h x 11w
**710** 14h x 2w
**711** 8h x 20w
**712** 3h x 18w
**713** 14h x 11w
**714** 8h x 6w
**715** 8h x 6w
**716** 8h x 6w
**717** 8h x 6w
**718** 56h x 20w
**719** 25h x 24w
**720** 20h x 10w
**721** 24h x 14w
**722** 16h x 17w
**723** 16h x 17w

**724** 16h x 12w
**725** 17h x 22w
**726** 16h x 16w
**727** 17h x 17w
**728** 12h x 17w
**729** 16h x 17w
**730** 15h x 15w
**731** 16h x 14w
**732** 8h x 19w
**733** 16h x 11w

**CHILDREN**
**734** 29h x 9w
**735** 26h x 32w
**736** 24h x 17w
**737** 24h x 29w
**738** 25h x 45w
**739** 20h x 43w
**740** 12h x 12w
**741** 12h x 12w
**742** 12h x 12w
**743** 12h x 12w
**744** 59h x 32w
**745** 24h x 21w
**746** 21h x 23w
**747** 31h x 31w
**748** 12w
**749** 11h
**750** 9h
**751** 3h
**752** 7h
**753** 12h
**754** 12h
**755** 15h
**756** 23h
**757** 33h x 32w
**758** 14h x 8w
**759** 14h x 8w
**760** 15h x 8w
**761** 15h x 8w
**762** 15h x 8w
**763** 15h x 8w
**764** 17h x 7w
**765** 17h x 7w
**766** 17h x 17w
**767** 20h
**768** 23h x 15w
**769** 16h
**770** 13h x 13w
**771** 14h x 30w
**772** 14h x 30w

**773** 28h x 43w
**774** 26h x 17w
**775** 26h x 17w
**776** 26h x 17w
**777** 26h x 17w
**778** 26h x 3w
**779** 26h x 3w
**780** 26h x 3w
**781** 26h x 3w
**782** 26h x 3w
**783** 26h x 3w
**784** 26h x 3w
**785** 26h x 3w
**786** 31h x 24w
**787** 4h x 24w
**788** 7h x 48w
**789** 11h x 31w
**790** 7h x 7w
**791** 1h x 7w
**793** 7h x 7w
**794** 31h x 24w
**795** 34h x 5w
**796** 8h x 8w
**797** 24h x 28w
**798** 24h x 19w
**799** 24h x 19w
**800** 32h x 26w
**801** 24h x 47w
**802** 11h
**803** 16h
**804** 42h x 38w
**805** 12h x 14w
**806** 12h x 14w
**807** 12h x 14w
**808** 35h x 27w
**809** 17h x 13w
**810** 12h x 13w
**811** 25h x 19w
**812** 40h x 42w
**813** 13h
**814** 40h x 42w
**815** 3h
**816** 9h

**GEOMETRIC**
**817** 3h
**818** 5h
**819** 5h
**820** 5h
**821** 3h
**822** 5h

**Fold out this flap to find an at-a-glance guide explaining how to use the charts in this book**

# READING A CHART

A cross stitch design is worked from a chart onto evenweave fabric by counting the blocks or threads in the fabric to position the stitches accurately. Each cross stitch is represented in this book by a colored cross occupying one block of fabric. Unfilled fabric blocks on a motif, letter, or border show the number of unworked blocks that separate groups of stitches. As a general rule, start stitching at the center of a cross stitch design, working outward from the center of the chart by working one complete cross stitch for every colored cross shown on the chart.

**FORMING THE STITCHES** Each cross can be formed exactly as shown above left, or the top and bottom diagonal stitches can be worked to slant in the opposite direction as shown above right. Whichever way you prefer to stitch, remember to be consistent, making sure the top diagonals of each cross slant in the same direction.

**STITCH COLOR KEY** A key runs across the top of each page and indicates which thread color should be used to stitch each cross shown on the chart. Fifty-eight colors are used throughout the book and each color is cross-referenced to both DMC and Anchor floss color numbers on pages 254.

**CATEGORY** The motifs are divided into 11 different themes.

**NUMBERS** Each motif is numbered and cross-referenced to the list of motif sizes at the back of the book.

**BACKGROUND GRID** To make counting easier, the background grid on each page is divided by thin black lines into blocks of five squares by five.

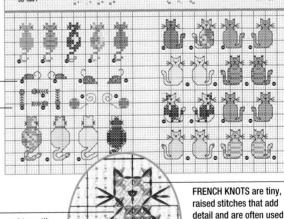

**BACKSTITCH LINES** are used to outline and define areas of cross stitch and these are shown as straight stitches on the charts.

**FRENCH KNOTS** are tiny, raised stitches that add detail and are often used to depict an eye on a bird or animal. They are shown on the charts as tiny solid dots.

| | | | | |
|---|---|---|---|---|
| **823** 3h | **874** 33h x 24w | **925** 25h x 25w | **977** 13h | **1028** 24h x 7w | **1076** 7h x 5w |
| **824** 9h | **875** 21h x 21w | **926** 18h x 18w | **978** 13h | **1029** 24h x 7w | **1077** 5h |
| **825** 4h | **876** 20h x 20w | **927** 8h x 8w | **979** 11h | **1030** 24h x 7w | **1078** 9h |
| **826** 6h | **877** 20h x 20w | **928** 8h x 8w | **980** 7h | **1031** 34h x 17w | **1079** 7h |
| **827** 9h | **878** 11h x 24w | **929** 8h x 8w | **981** 15h | **1032** 19h x 9w | **1080** 7h |
| **828** 8h | **879** 21h x 21w | **930** 8h x 8w | **982** 12h | **1033** 19h x 9w | **1081** 7h |
| **829** 8h | **880** 15h x 23w | **931** 17h x 17w | **983** 11h | **1034** 19h x 9w | **1082** 5h |
| **830** 8h | **881** 13h x 20w | **932** 8h x 8w | **984** 27h | **1035** 19h x 9w | **1083** 5h |
| **831** 3h | **882** 33h x 25w | **933** 8h x 8w | **985** 15h | **1036** 19h x 9w | **1084** 7h |
| **832** 5h | **883** 20h x 20w | **934** 8h x 8w | **986** 10h | **1037** 19h x 9w | **1085** 3h x 3w |
| **833** 5h | **884** 10h x 10w | **935** 32h x 32w | **987** 3h | **1038** 19h x 9w | **1086** 7h |
| **834** 5h | **885** 10h x 10w | **936** 10h | **988** 11h | **1039** 19h x 9w | **1087** 13h |
| **835** 5h | **886** 10h x 10w | **937** 12h | **989** 3h | **1040** 12h | **1088** 13h x 13w |
| **836** 5h | **887** 10h x 10w | **938** 7h | **990** 17h | **1041** 21h x 15w | **1089** 11h x 11w |
| **837** 5h | **888** 8h x 8w | **939** 17h | **991** 17h | **1042** 20h x 17w | **1090** 13h x 13w |
| **838** 5h | **889** 8h x 8w | **940** 11h | **992** 16h | **1043** 31h x 7w | **1091** 13h x 13w |
| **839** 3h | **890** 8h x 8w | **941** 5h | **993** 8h | **1044** 19h x 9w | **1092** 13h x 13w |
| **840** 4h | **891** 8h x 8w | **942** 11h | **994** 8h | **1045** 19h x 9w | **1093** 10h |
| **841** 4h | **892** 19h x 19w | **943** 9h | **995** 13h | **1046** 19h x 11w | **1094** 9h x 5w |
| **842** 4h | **893** 19h x 19w | **944** 5h | **996** 17h | **1047** 10h | **1095** 7h |
| **843** 4h | **894** 19h x 19w | | **997** 12h | **1048** 23h x 7w | **1096** 13h |
| **844** 6h | **895** 19h x 19w | **SAMPLERS** | **998** 13h | **1049** 12h x 23w | **1097** 14h |
| **845** 5h | **896** 19h x 19w | **945** 2h | **999** 10h | **1050** 5h x 5w | **1098** 7h x 42w |
| **846** 4h | **897** 19h x 19w | **946** 2h | **1000** 11h | **1051** 12h x 13w | **1099** 8h x 49w |
| **847** 2h | **898** 19h x 19w | **947** 3h | **1001** 14h | **1052** 4h x 5w | **1100** 7h x 20w |
| **848** 10h | **899** 19h x 19w | **948** 5h | **1002** 10h | **1053** 12h x 13w | **1101** 11h |
| **849** 8h | **900** 19h x 19w | **949** 6h | **1003** 12h | **1054** 15h x 28w | **1102** 3h |
| **850** 8h | **901** 8h | **950** 5h | **1004** 11h | **1055** 5h x 9w | **1103** 3h |
| **851** 11h | **902** 8h | **951** 4h | **1005** 33h x 27w | **1056** 22h x 46w | **1104** 5h |
| **852** 10h | **903** 12h | **952** 4h | **1006** 17h x 17w | **1057** 5h x 15w | **1105** 3h |
| **853** 13h | **904** 22h | **953** 3h | **1007** 21h x 23w | **1058** 5h x 15w | **1106** 3h |
| **854** 13h | **905** 26h x 26w | **954** 8h | **1008** 21h x 23w | **1059** 36h x 47w | **1107** 5h |
| **855** 13h | **906** 14h x 14w | **955** 2h | **1009** 7h x 23w | **1060** 20h x 47w | **1108** 5h |
| **856** 8h | **907** 14h x 14w | **956** 5h | **1010** 29h x 19w | | **1109** 14h |
| **857** 25h x 25w | **908** 7h x 7w | **957** 5h | **1011** 29h x 11w | **ALPHABETS** | **1110** 16h |
| **858** 15h x 21w | **909** 17h x 20w | **958** 7h | **1012** 30h x 11w | **AND NUMBERS** | |
| **859** 15h x 21w | **910** 8h x 8w | **959** 4h | **1013** 26h x 17w | **1061** 4h | |
| **860** 30h x 25w | **911** 8h x 8w | **960** 8h | **1014** 26h x 7w | **1062** 3h | |
| **861** 41h x 21w | **912** 9h x 49w | **961** 3h | **1015** 26h x 17w | **1063** 5h | |
| **862** 32h x 48w | **913** 5h x 19w | **962** 7h | **1016** 14h x 17w | **1064** 4h | |
| **863** 25h x 49w | **914** 25h x 25w | **963** 6h | **1017** 15h x 17w | **1065** 5h | |
| **864** 15h x 21w | **915** 15h x 15w | **964** 5h | **1018** 7h x 5w | **1066** 4h | |
| **865** 15h x 21w | **916** 13h x 19w | **968** 4h | **1019** 30h x 27w | **1067** 4h | |
| **866** 21h x 21w | **917** 22h x 22w | **969** 6h | **1020** 8h x 5w | **1068** 5h | |
| **867** 36h x 21w | **918** 22h x 22w | **970** 8h | **1021** 6h x 27w | **1069** 4h | |
| **868** 20h x 23w | **919** 7h | **971** 7h | **1022** 11h x 13w | **1070** 5h | |
| **869** 28h x 21w | **920** 47h x 47w | **972** 7h | **1023** 11h x 13w | **1071** 9h | |
| **870** 15h x 25w | **921** 28h x 28w | **973** 7h | **1024** 24h x 17w | **1072** 8h | |
| **871** 10h x 25w | **922** 11h x 11w | **974** 10h | **1025** 17h x 23w | **1073** 10h | |
| **872** 28h x 28w | **923** 5h x 5w | **975** 6h | 1026 23h x 21w | **1074** 5h x 3w | |
| **873** 28h x 14w | **924** 17h x 17w | **976** 19h | **1027** 10h x 25w | **1075** 7h | |

# THREAD CONVERSION CHART

| Key number and name | DMC thread | Anchor thread | Key number and name | DMC thread | Anchor thread |
|---|---|---|---|---|---|
| 1 white | blanc | 2 | 30 royal blue | 797 | 132 |
| 2 black | 310 | 403 | 31 dark Delft blue | 798 | 146 |
| 3 very dark pewter grey | 3799 | 236 | 32 Delft blue | 809 | 130 |
| 4 dark steel grey | 414 | 235 | 33 very light violet-blue | 3747 | 120 |
| 5 pearl grey | 415 | 398 | 34 dark electric blue | 995 | 410 |
| 6 very dark mocha brown | 3031 | 905 | 35 medium electric blue | 996 | 433 |
| 7 medium beige-brown | 840 | 1084 | 36 light Wedgwood | 518 | 1039 |
| 8 medium light antique gold | 832 | 907 | 37 medium light peacock blue | 376 | 167 |
| 9 medium light beige-grey | 644 | 830 | 38 very light sky blue | 747 | 158 |
| 10 ecru | ecru | 387 | 39 very dark sea green | 3812 | 188 |
| 11 very light old gold | 677 | 886 | 40 medium peacock green | 959 | 186 |
| 12 dark golden brown | 975 | 355 | 41 dark violet-blue | 333 | 119 |
| 13 medium golden brown | 976 | 1001 | 42 dark violet | 552 | 99 |
| 14 bright Christmas red | 666 | 46 | 43 medium lavender | 210 | 108 |
| 15 bright orange | 608 | 332 | 44 light lavender | 211 | 342 |
| 16 light tangerine | 742 | 303 | 45 hunter green | 3346 | 267 |
| 17 dark lemon | 444 | 290 | 46 light pistachio green | 368 | 214 |
| 18 very light topaz | 727 | 293 | 47 light yellow-green | 3348 | 264 |
| 19 very dark dusty rose | 150 | 59 | 48 very dark emerald green | 3818 | 923 |
| 20 cranberry | 603 | 62 | 49 dark emerald green | 910 | 230 |
| 21 very light dusty rose | 151 | 73 | 50 Kelly green | 702 | 226 |
| 22 light carnation | 893 | 27 | 51 bright chartreuse | 704 | 256 |
| 23 very light carnation | 894 | 26 | 52 very dark blue-green | 500 | 683 |
| 24 very light salmon | 3713 | 1020 | 53 dark celadon green | 3815 | 877 |
| 25 salmon | 760 | 1022 | 54 light blue-green | 503 | 876 |
| 26 very light terracotta | 3779 | 868 | 55 dark Christmas red | 498 | 1005 |
| 27 very light peach flesh | 948 | 1011 | 56 pale pumpkin | 3825 | 323 |
| 28 medium dark navy blue | 336 | 150 | 57 light copper | 922 | 1003 |
| 29 very dark blue | 824 | 164 | 58 dark garnet | 814 | 45 |

# Web resources

## MANUFACTURERS

**Coats Crafts UK**: www.coatscrafts.co.uk
Anchor threads and Jobelan fabric.

**DMC**: www.dmc.com
DMC threads and cross stitch fabrics; information
and stockists

**Mill Hill**: www.millhillbeads.com
Glass seed beads

## UK STOCKISTS

**Willow Fabrics**: www.willowfabrics.com

**Zweigart fabrics**: Aida, even-weave and linen
fabrics; embroidery threads including Anchor, Caron
Collection, Au Ver á Soie, Kreinik

**Cross Stitch Direct**: www.stitchdirect.co.uk
DMC and other fabrics; embroidery threads
including Anchor, DMC, Caron Collection, Rainbow
Gallery; Mill Hill Beads

**Tandem Cottage**: www.threadsite.co.uk/tandem/
Embroidery fabrics and threads including Anchor,
DMC, Madeira

**West End Embroidery**: www.westendembroidery.
co.uk
A wide range of threads including The Gentle Art,
Caron Collection, Weeks Dye Works, Needle
Necessities, Thread Gatherer, Rainbow Gallery; Mill
Hill Beads

## GRAPH PAPER
Downloadable shareware software to print out
customized graph paper
www.marquis-soft.com/graphpapeng.htm

# Index

# Credits

All illustrations and photographs are the copyright of Quarto Publishing plc. While every effort has been made to credit contributors, Quarto would like to apologize should there have been any omissions or errors—and would be pleased to make the appropriate correction for future editions of the book.